The Siege of Acre by Hannah Cowley

Hannah Cowley was born Hannah Parkhouse on March 14th, 1743, the daughter of Hannah (née Richards) and Philip Parkhouse, a bookseller in Tiverton, Devon.

As one might expect details of much of her life are scant and that of her early life almost non-existent.

However, we do know that she married Thomas Cowley and that the couple moved to London where Thomas worked as an official in the Stamp Office and as a part-time journalist.

Her career in the literary world seemed to happen rather late. It was whilst the couple were attending a play, thought to be sometime in late 1775, that Cowley was struck by a sudden necessity to write.

Her first play, a comedy called The Runaway was sent to the famed actor-manager, David Garrick. It was produced at his final season at the Drury Lane theatre on February 15th, 1776. It was a success. She wrote her next two plays, the farce, Who's the Dupe? and the tragedy, Albina, before the year was out.

Getting these two plays into production took much longer and involved a very public spat with her rival Hannah More over whether Cowley's works had been plagarised by More.

Cowley wrote her most popular comedy in 1780; The Belle's Stratagem. It was staged at Covent Garden.

Her next play, The World as It Goes; or, a Party at Montpelier (the title was later changed to Second Thoughts Are Best) was unsuccessful, but she continued to write and there followed another seven plays; Which is the Man?; A Bold Stroke for a Husband; More Ways Than One; A School for Greybeards, or, The Mourning Bride; The Fate of Sparta, or, The Rival Kings; A Day in Turkey, or, The Russian Slaves and The Town Before You.

In 1801 Cowley published perhaps her greatest poetical work. A six-book epic "The Siege of Acre: An Epic Poem".

That same year Cowley retired to Tiverton in Devon, where she spent her remaining years out of the public spotlight whilst she quietly revised her plays.

Hannah Cowley died of liver failure on March 11th, 1809.

Index of Contents
Book I
Book II
Book III
Book IV
Book V
Book VI
Hannah Cowley – A Short Biography
Hannah Cowley – A Concise Bibliography

BOOK I

"Weave the Crimson Web of War
"Let us go and let us fly
"Where our friends the conflict share,
"Where they triumph, where they died'

Blest Art thou!
Blest by whatsoever name,
Who warm'st my heart, and breath'st o'er all my Frame!
Art thou THE MUSE whose presence thus I greet,
Whose cheering presence makes lone hours so sweet?
Art thou the Muse? Ah no! for FICTION She,
Celestial Truth! I seize the theme from Thee!
Be thou the Guardian of my page, Firm Maid,
And through thy shining fields thy Vot'ry aid:
Yet GODDESS! in thy train be found the Fair,

With rosy pinions, and refulgent hair —
Imagination; O, the Nymph be thine!
Let her bright stole around thy bosom twine,
Her blooming Chaplet on thy brow be bound,
Thy Ivory shape her sparkling zone surround;
Thus deck'd, amidst thy Scenes detain me long,
Controul my verse and vindicate my song!

ACRE! thou little tributary Spot,
Wond'rous thy fortune, and sublime thy Lot!
Immortal lustre to thy name is given,
O! graced by Nature, aggrandized by Heaven!
Thou wert The Chosen from the nations round,
To gallic Madness an imperious bound;
"Here shalt thou stop the sacred Fiat said,
Th' Apostate shrunk—his martial Legions bled.
Acre! 'twas thine to bid the victor fear,
To turn him; in the flush of his career!
He, who o'er Asia meant to drag the fight,
And at Byzantium all his horrors light,
Through Hungary to force a sanguine way,
And in Vienna hail Rebellion's day,
Back, through the gasping country sought the road —
O'er which triumphantly so late he strode;
O'er hopeless Vasts, and solitudes of fire,
Bowed down by shame, reluctant they retire:
Thine ACRE was the check; the Deed was thine,
In Europe's annals, grateful let it shine!

The Means how small, weighed with the mighty End;
A Handful, from thy walls whole Legions send,
But these were English—They were ENGLISH TARS,
Kings of the Sea, and Gods in Syria's Wars!

THE CONQUEROR OF ITALY (dread name!
Bestowed upon the Chief by gallic fame)
Returned from classic Tyber's flow'ry shores,
To where the Seine its muddy confluence pours.
What though the Tyber in poetic song,
Hath Ages rolled a dazzling flood along;
Though Roman Poets struck the sounding Lyre,
And caught beneath its Sun enduring fire,
Yet will the muddy Seine eclipse its name,
Or roll an equal tide, and own an equal fame.
WONDERS burst daily o'er its sluggish wave,
And fresh anomalies stern REASON brave,
Anterior lights assist no more her Eye,
And modem facts her grave deductions fly;
Hist'ry astonished will the acts engrave,
Which freed a Nation, and its Sons enslave.

FROM the proud plains which erst? the Caesars trod,
The Warrior led the bands the French bestow'd;
In their own Capital their Arms were piled,
Trophies adorn'd, and Fetes the hours beguiled.
Soothed with the pleasant race his glory ran,
New Bays, new Trophies, his rapt Fancy spun,
To fruitful Egypt flew his ardent thought
Where Rome had conquer'd, and where Greece had fought
The COUNCIL caught the plan, a Fleet decreed,
And to their station distant vessels speed,
From ev'ry Bay they croud th' incumber'd Wave,
And all the watchful force of England brave,
Whose NAVAL CITIES belt Earth's monstrous Round,
And lift their Spires wherever Ocean's found.
ENGLAND! O, give thy science, powers, strength to THESE
The Earth is thine, whilst Mistress of its Seas!
Bid foreign Forests seek thy mighty Docks,
Tear ductile metal from thy native rocks,
From thy waste Lands bid all thy Cables spring,
And their rough sinews midst the Ocean fling—
Scorn FRANCE! their wiles, their diplomatic Arts,
Thy NAVY 'll break their spells; thy NAVY 'll bow their hearts!

NOT to be rash, and to make certain SURE,
The Chief resolved fresh labours to endure,
To midnight lamps his anxious hours resigned,

And books and battles share his mighty mind:
Whilst Paris danc'd, or in the tribune roar'd,
He round him called a literary horde:
In breathing forms philosophy he read,
Nor only books, nor only musty Dead;
Living and Dead his genius knew to prize,
The fops of learning, and the really wise;
Antients and moderns he alike perused,
Devouring all th' unburden'd press diffused
On Syria's Citadels, and Egypt's plains,
The route of Philip's Son, and Antony's campaigns.

Thus, when towards the Sea his forces drew,
Bidding to tortured Europe an adieu,
Globes, Maps, and Travels, ev'ry Waggon bore,
And plans of fortresses an ample store,
Sg avails and Heroes were filed off by Troops,
Here Soldiers march'd; there, volume writing Groupes
What could impede a scheme thus sagely plann'd?
POETS, PHILOSOPHERS, his purpose fann'd!

HISTORIC MAID! descend not thou to smile,
Nor steal thy Sister's light, sarcastic style,
Assume thy air chastised thy sober Mien,
And move with serious dignity, A QUEEN,
Let grave composure mark thy steady pace,
And glide around thee with a matron grace!

THE flower of every band the Gen'ral chose,
Fresh, from the flush of Victory they rose,
Their brows wore triumph, menace in their tread,
And all seem'd Conq'rers,—by a Conq'rer led!
Born midst a stranger race, a stranger tongue,
He guides not those to fight 'mongst whom he sprung
Not linked to those for whom he Empires claims,
No PATRIOT FLAME gives grandeur to his aims;
Yet high in fame, and by his troops ador'd,
He leads them at his will—resistless Lord!
Mild in his Manners, gracious in his Mien,
To win his Camp he needs but to be seen;
He knows the Warrior's and the Sage's part,
In Council thoughtful, in the field a dart!
Forth from Toulon's wide Bay the Pilots steer,
Their fleet brings graceful out it's length'ning rear,
Straight through the wat'ry Empire, to the East,
'They onward press; with fervid hopes increas'd,
Yet soon seduced the mighty Squadron veer'd,
Swift, at the signal, helms obedient steer'd.

Her snowy plumage, bending midst the waves
Of palace bordered Thames, the tall swan laves,
Stately she sits Upon the gentle tide,
Whilst o'er her form the lines of beauty glide—
As white, as stately, as the cumbent Swan
When mildest winds her glossy feathers fan,
Rose, midst the tumid billows MALTA'S Spires,
Her marble Cities and her gilded Quires.

Instant around her ports their pennons float,
Almost her dazzling Shores their bowsprits smote
Short and acute the struggle which ensued,
Her rocks of snowy hue with blood imbued,
Soon saw the baleful TREE insult the ground,
And heard the horrid triumph leap around—.
Near the green hedges thus, on Summer nights;
The twinkling glow-worm all its beauties lights,
A living jewel the soft insect seems,
And paints with varied tint it's dang'rous beams
To itself dangerous, the bird of prey
Beholds its clear, enticing, starry ray—,
Inbred the foe which lures him from the Skies,
Swift he descends, and in his: grasp it dies!
Inbred the enemies of Malta's Land;
As the French prows approach'd her peaceful
Strand In her own Towns, Sedition raised his arm
And REVOLUTION sounded the alarm;
Less conquer'd than, obtain'd, the Island fell,
For there no more her Knights with courage swell;
Afric's Stern Sons no more their Thunders tame,
Nor Asia bends before their awful name.

FROM Malta loos'd, the shouting Fleet proceeds
To greater objects, to more daring deeds;
The fav'ring winds within their canvas play,
Their wishes, winds and waves alike, obey,
No hurricane deforms the Ocean's glass,
Which spreads its plain more level as they pass,
The softest Zephyrs through the cordage sing
And flutter midst their flags with silken wing.—
Like those which heretofore on Egypt's coast
(Of classic pens the subject and the boast)
Swell'd the soft Sails of the Circean Queen,
Whilst a lost Emperor disgraced the Scene,
A new Italian Hero ploughs the waves,
And Egypt's Sea his hostile Vessel braves;
He springs upon her Land with ardent feet,
And her low Shores ten thousand voices greet!

Four times ten thousand did the ranks contain
Whose feet smote Egypt from the frothy Main.

QUEEN OF THE SOUTH! thy cluster'd Mountains gush,
Forth from their Caverns Floods and Rivers rush,
Seeking the sacred stream whose Magic lave,
Bids Harvests burst from its descending wave,
From its thick slime sees Bowers and Groves arise,
The Sands drink deep and blush with healthful dyes
The stranger streams each gasping root embrace,
And to the Desart's edge push shade, and grace.
Each russet stem mount up, its buds unfold,
Its silver blossoms and its Orbs of gold,
With dulcet acid swell the Lemon's sides,
And through high Myrtles force the em'rald tides
Ascend with syphon powers the giant Palm,
To Roses otto give, and gum to balm.
Rejoiced, the liquid Wilderness beholds,
And grasps glad nations in its shining folds.
In vain, fair SHEBA! vain thy glutted Nile
Bade Egypt flourish, and her Delta smile:—
THESE came like Pests of Locusts o'er her fields,
Swarm'd o'er the fruits her sultry climate yields,
Her orange woods, her citrons swell'd in vain,
Or swell'd, invading legions to sustain.
Her humid fields of grain—the icey seed,
Which the fierce Sun and burning Dog Star breed,
The plunging hoofs of cavalry surprise,
And as they pour along, the Summer dies.

To sage Futurity be left their road!
Her page shall shew how swift the Earth they trod;
Of Arab battles, triumphs, flights, she'll tell,
What sieges stay'd them, and what cities fell:
The Towers of PTOLEMAIS command the Muse
Where bleeding valleys every joy refuse,
Where the hoarse Trumpet's blast is heard from far,
Compelling SYRIA to, defensive War,
The Tygers of the War, bounding proceed,
And SYRIA'S CONQUEST boldly is decreed;
They dare the ills of every orient Sand,
Springing with fury o'er the Scorching Land,
The Serpents of the Desart hiss in vain,
Nor red Simooms with pestilence restrain,
But ere they came—Recording Time! the day
Illustrate ever with thy brightest ray Is
HE, sent by England to resist the War,
And with firm arm the views of France to mar,

With floating Citadels approach'd the Coast,
And cloath'd its borders with his naval host;
Spirits from heaven they seem'd, who breathed in fire,
Whilst the touch'd Syrians, kindred warmth respire,
Rise into Heroes as the Britons tread,
And, in their paths, emerging Laurels spread.
Scarce the Commander had his anchor bound
Within th' unsteady Haven's rocky ground,
Ere at MOUNT CARMEL'S base (whose slope descends
Where Acre's river widi the wide Sea blends)
The foe's presumptuous transports steady move,
And dauntless on the Syriac Ocean rove;
With haughty stripes triumphantly unfurl'd,
They flash'd defiance o'er the wat'ry World.

THE dragon-fly self-pois'd on sparkling wings,
His tap'ring body braced by golden rings,
Swims through the eddying air with mazy pride,
And lends his beauties to th' etherial tide;
The trusted tide beats him with headlong force,
Where the stretch'd throat arrests his fluent course;
He sees the gaping gulph but sees too late,
And darts on sparkling pinions to his fate.
So glitt'ring pendants floated o'er the surge,
And fraudful winds French sails impetuous urge—
Important moment! on the raptured glance
Of watchful BRITONS swiftly they advance;
Instant the TIGRE weigh'd; her powerful Guns
Arrest the veering fleet, which prudent runs;
The THESEUS aided the Commander's plan,
Corvettes and Transports soon no longer ran;—
SEVEN CAPTURED VESSELS in old Acre's Bay,
Seem'd but a Summer Eve's heroic play
But ah! not play was found their, glorious freight,
Vast Carronades, Mortars of monstrous weight
To batter Acre's Towers the vessels bore,
And implements of War—profuse the store!
To Acre its DEFENCE they blindly bring,
And shouts of welcome through the Fortress, ring;
Whilst slow descended from Mount Carmel's height,
Soft shadows, tinted with departing light.
What misty folds once wrapp'd its palmy head,
The holy, penman's hallow'd page hath said:
When Baal's Priests THE MIGHTY SEER commands
Their God to invocate with impious hands.
There, on the altar lay a youthful Bull,
His veins with rapid spirits late were full,
Prince of the herd! white was his glossy hide,

His ivory horns with blushing flow'rs were tied.
ELIJAH pour'd upon each quiv'ring part,
The frowning head and palpitating heart,
The brook translucent. "Pour again," he cried,
"Be ev'ry vessel copiously supplied;
"Fill yet your urns! let the surrounding trough
"Drink the soft tide, till ev'ry trench o'erflow!
"O! that the Ocean all its Deeps would raise,
"In honour of the God whose name WE praise!
Obeyed, the Prophet breathed an ardent prayer,
Whilst downward darting through the steady air.
Pale sheety light upon the Altar came,
And all was instant lost in dazzling flame,
The foaming waters kiss'd the sacred fire,
Fed the pure flame and bade it fierce aspire;
White scented vapours from the trenches rose.
Spread o'er the Mount, and all its Groves enclose,
Samaria's King and warring Chariot's veil,
And Israel's doubting faithless Son conceal.
The Priests of Baal shriek; own JUDAH'S GOD,
And vainly fly from, the avenging rod;
The regal Ahab shrunk upon his throne,
His fear-struck heart forgot its impious tone,
He, and his trembling Warriors homeward turn,
Whilst yet the vapours mount, the trenches burn!

Now, constellations hung their chains of light,
Guiding o'er Acre's towers the vernal Night;
The bending LINE unfolds its graceful road,
And for the Nymph its brightest gems were strew'd;
Each air was hush'd as came the placid Queen,
And silence gave soft int'rest to the Scene,
Fresh dews condens'd to form her fleecy Car,
Rolling on axles of pellucid spar.
She shook her veil;—its edges poppies graced,
Pale as the milky zonfe which bound her waist—
From all its borders balmy slumbers slide,
And to the Syrian pillows gently glide,
With sweet compulsion bade each eye-lid close,
And threw around the spells of deep repose.
Yet did THE SOUNDS OF TRIUMPH tingle still,
And by enchantment ev'ry organ fill,
Giving to sleep itself a powerful zest,
Thrilling the Soul, yet not suspending rest.
Thus pass'd the hours the soothing Queen bestow'd,
Till through the air the tints of Morning glow'd,
Each Warrior sprung to meet the florid ray,
And martial greetings hail'd th' approaching Day.

Corslets and Sabres in a moment placed,
And Scimeters hang curving from the waist;
In their own Æther long lost feathers wave,
And borne on Helmets indicate the BRAVE—
Thus in stern War's transmuting limbec bound,
Softness itself darts aweful terrors round,
A Death seems peeping through each downy flake,
And his full quiver trembles as they shake.

DOWN like a torrent tumbling o'er a Rock,
Giving the country round a trem'lous shock,
From Syria's Mountains rush'd th' impending foe,
And spread upon the ripen'd vales below
Hot with vile massacre, with carnage red,
More than Wars terrors hail them as they tread;
The polish'd General of the Tuscan plains
Wore here a Dastard's heart, a Ruffian's stains.
O! glorious, wicked, virtuous, wondrous Man,
Whose Prototype no History can scan,
Whom to repeat shall future ages foil,
Monster! to baffle NATURE wherefore toil?
Ah! know'st Thou not that when she framed thy Soul,
She bade PERFECTION seal the lustrous Whole?
She bade! Religion raised its towering Wing,
Scorn'd the command, and with an upward spring
Left incomplete, what Nature longed to see,
Who trembling, gave her fav'rite Planet, THEE!
So, when the storied Thetis flew to lave
Her Godlike Son in th' indurating Wave,
One vulnerable Tendon still was found,
One peccant spot—t' invite the deadly wound,
The peccant spot mock'd all her matron care,
And Gifts Divine were lost upon her Heir.

JAFFA subdued, bade the dire Battle cease
Three days her Sons had rest, and. all was Peace!!
But oh! their Foes they had opposed in fight—
OMNIPOTENCE itself bestow'd the right,
The right to MAN to guard his Laws, and Lands,
From fierce Invasion's desolating hands;
When Nations first sprung forth the right began,
A higher Duty scarce belongs to Man!
Thus, the third day amidst their quiet streets,
FRENCH MURDERERS each loyal Townsman meets;
And half the Butcheries of Paris rise
Before astonish'd Asia's tortured Eyes.
Proud of these acts, they sent their fame before,
And prompt Report the tragic story bore;

It floated through the Coast—the pop'lous vale,
Whilst Horror triumph'd at the brutal tale.
THEY CAME! They swept across the arid Plain,
With fateful Engines rolling in their train;
Then winding to an insulated Mound,
Their Camp hung sudden on its rising ground.

THE chosen Hill had Ocean in its View,
And o'er its Slope the Winds salubrious flew,
Here they reposed, screen'd from the torrid glow,
Incautious of the Ills which lurk'd below!
Scarce had they mark'd the Lines, form'd every Street,
And saw the Hexagon its form compleat,
Ere from the English Ships intol'rant fire,
Bade the astonish'd Corsican retire.
His vast Marquee, with long drawn suite is down,
Prostrate the Streets, banish'd the canvass Town;—
Morgana's Cities meltless fleet away,
Whilst wond'ring Naples crowds her silver Bay!
The Seamen, hooting, saw th' Invaders speed,
And laugh, and wit Marine their rout succeed.
A Hill more distant the Besiegers scale,
Which feath'ring rose enormous o'er the dale,
Thence their high Camp obtruded on the eye,
Seeming to threaten Acre from the sky;
In Abyssinia thus when Battle pours,
Hang clouds of Vultures o'er her threaten'd Towers.

THE open'd Gates the Corsican demands,
He found sustain'd by firm and haughty bands.
ACHMET PASHAW whose life of oft told years,
On his wan brow and sunken Eye appears,
Whate'er the crimes or virtues of his heart,
From an insulting foe disdain'd to start.
THE SIEGE BEGAN in all its horrid form,
War flings its lightnings and awakes the Storm!
Untir'd, the Echoes of its thunders roll,
Start from the Line, and vibrate at the Pole;
Load the meek Zephyrs of the humid Vale,
Sieze the strong pinions of the Mountain gale,
The tale of blood to peaceful regions bear,
And give to SAFETY'S Couch th'e thrill of fear.
Close to the Beech the English Ships were moor'd,
And o'er the Foe their CAPTURED Cannon roar'd;
Well poised, each bore upon the Gallic flank,
Hurling Destruction through a prostrate rank:
Thus on themselves their own dread thunders fall',
And FRANCE, destroys her Sons at Acre's Wall!

AT Acre's Wall her Powers innum'rous shone,
Yet not in popularity alone,
Stood they superior to their turban'd foes,
Whose fire by tactic art unaided, glows,
They boasted Engineers of valued skill,
Warm from the Schools, VAUB AN'S sage volumes fill,
These Science-taught, insidious path-ways form'd
Whilst o'er their Necks the battlements were storm'd.
Beneath the Town they work'd a dreary road
Where seeds of future fires were to be stow'd—
Such fires as bursting through the ribs of Earth
Destroy a World whilst struggling into birth!
The startled Gnomes, wrapt in Primeval rest,
In dark security supremely blest,
From the young hour in which their Orb arose
Amidst confusion, and chaotic throes,
Abhorr'd the GAUDY MONSTER of the sky,
Who bids his burning beams through Æther fly.
The ray, the Mole's fine vision twilight deem'd,
To GNOMES, meridian bursts of splendor seem'd,
Such pow'rful floods of Glory dimm'd their sight,
And their nerves deaden'd in excessive light!
But now, when real twilight glimmer'd through,
They shrieking, from the dreadful flame withdrew,
Pierced the thick Earth, swift as a winged thought,
And in her central Domes, her deepest shadows sought;
There, 'midst the Diamond's blaze their sports they keep,
And, where the ruby lights its torch they sleep —
Sigh for the wretched fate which Mortals know,
Condemn'd to breathe in Domes where Day beams glow!

RAPID the Miners work, their Engines groan.
Now sinking deep, now horizont'ly prone;
Still more remote from faintest light they go,
'Till far behind its scintillations flow,
When unexpected visions blazed around,
And ENGLAND'S WARRIORS start from forth the ground,
Burst with their glitt'ring arms upon the sight,
And pour dread radiance through these realms of night.
Foil'd thus by counter-works, th' Invaders fled,
Daring 'midst living Graves to yield to dread!
The shouting ENGLISH through each turn pursue,
And trace the Labyrinth—their Foe their clue;
The Labyrinth of DEATH it well were named,
For here the savage battle tugg'd untamed,
In a new form its horrid rites were given,
Remote from Man, and only seen by Heaven—.

Keeping their way the French unearth'd appear,
The galling Britons close upon the rear;
Thus through a sudden fissure Nature makes,
When the globe shivers, and the Mountain quakes,
By central force impell'd black waters rise,
And o'er the Land the spatt'ring mischief flies,
Subdues the harvest, deluges the grain,
The pasture darkens, and defiles the plain!

BATTLE thus smote our Orb each fearful day,
Near the soft Ides of gently breathing May;
Ah Month! so mild, so young, so fair to view,
Deck'd out in flowers, in scents, and sparkling dew,
Why did thy violated Groves complain,
Why wert thou called such horrors to sustain?
Th' astonish'd foe turn to their camp each night,
And each new Morn wake raging for the fight,
With bolder nerves re-seek the stubborn field,
Which frontless Brav'ry still refused to yield;
Which yet presumptuously the Arms withstand,
That hurl'd Destruction, o'er each struggling Land.
Benumb'd at length, their conquest they delay,
And 'midst their Camp inert and sullen stray;
Plan future glory; future ruin swear,
To those who bravely, insolently dare.
The EQUINOCTIAL FURY of the East,
Meanwhile bestrode her many-winged Beast;
Each hand sustain'd a dark reverted Urn,
From which at pleasure, as she chose, to turn,
Through the wide atmosphere they send their blasts,
And o'er the Earth opposing storms she casts.
Swift, she descended through the misty air,
And as she pass'd, she stripp'd each forest bare;
Down to the Ocean headlong then she drives,
And 'midst the mighty waters frantic dives,
Heaps up the billows to an Alpine's height,
And instant sinks them with destructive might;
The giddy Ships like tops she whirls around,
Now high they hang in air, now drop profound.
In Acre's rocky Bay no anchor holds,
The Cables coil'd, each Deck sustains the folds,
Far from the Shore the ENGLISH CAPTAIN driv'n,
To the wide Sea, his fleet and crews are giv'n!

Now rose the French again—they rose in strength.
ACRE! they cried, thy hour is come at length,
Whilst to the Deep thy vain Protectors go
We'll crush thee with a last decisive blow!

On, as inspired, they rush'd towards the Towers,
And their waked rage with doubled ardor pours:
But those within were now with lessons fraught,
Bestow'd by courage, or which life had bought;
No trophy lost, no haughty standards fall,
But blazing Crescents stream along the Wall.
It seem'd that British fire (so well they fought)
Ran through their veins'; for oft they boldly sought
Without the Gate the Gauls upon the Plain,
And higher martial power each day attain.
When coop'd within their long enduring Town,
In ev'ry mode defensive wrath came down,
By fury nerv'd, standing aloft they throw;
The pond'rous masses tumble on the foe.
The neighb'ring Mounts their marble contents yield,
Their marble contents bound upon the field—
Not harmless bound, each bears a wound along,
Nor falls unaimd upon the shrinking throng;
The thin air cleft murm'ring and hoarse it sings,
And round the whizzing murder, sighing clings;—
Thus ACRE fed with blood its parch'd up plain,
Thus travel'd FRANCE, the distant Globe to stain!

BOOK II

"Defend the Castle, guard the Gate!
"A moment lost's a day too late."

BUT who was He, who like a castled Rock,
Withstood the Battle's most intemp'rate Shock?
Dark was his visage, and his eye, all beam,
Emitted round a soul appalling gleam:
Th' Invaders rushing round him, fell like flowers
When darts the North's keen blast, its arrowy showers
Where'er he moved, his Scimeter was seen,
Whirling aloft its edge, or dropping keen;
No Helmet its descending force withstood,
The breast it struck pour'd forth a crimson flood,
Then to a Mount with winged speed he'd fly,
And from its summit throw his eagle eye
Across the War; mark where the French gave way,
Or where seem'd shrunk the Fortune of the day,
Then 'midst the Foe again the Hero stood,
And bore down all—a fierce o'erwhelming flood.
Say Muse! whilst now the hours of rest and night,
Bind with soft chains the Demons of the fight—

Say who the Man, that, in himself a band,
Opposed Invasion on the Syrian Strand?

HE, thus exalted 'midst the brave, and bold,
Ere the red War its horrid Engines roll'd,
Wedded the rich Abdallah's lovely heir,
Pre-eminent amidst the Syrian fair!
Since blaz'd the hours of their connubial Morn,
Three Moons had o'er the Earth their torches borne,
When Acre's Bulwarks and its feeble Towers,
Felt the first fury of Invading Powers.
OSMYN, disdaining all but patriot fire,
Trod the high Rartiparts, fill'd with sacred ire;
And where He saw his brave compatriots fall,
The BRIDEGROOM rush'd—the Guardian of the Wall!
Vain were soft IRA'S tears—for HER he fought;
And when her Father's tender nature caught
The soft infection of his Daughter's fears,
Vain were his prayers, as lovely Ira's tears!
Osmyn, all Soldier, in his lofty Soul
Confessed a fire nought human coifid controul.
Each Eve returning from the batter'd Towers,
(When to their Camp the foe led off their powers)
He smil'd at all the terrors she confest,
And laugh'd at Danger, and her fears supprest.
Of painless wounds like Roman Arria feign'd;—
His soul to. Glory's highest pitch was strain'd,
And as he spoke of Death, and War, and Arms,
The subject gave fresh lustre to his charms:
IRA enamour'd hung upon the sounds,
And caught disdain for Death, and painless wounds.
At length she grew familiar with the theme—
O! female weakness ever in extreme!
No longer shudder'd as the cannon roar'd,
Nor shrunk in thought from the uplifted Sword.
The Eaglet thus amidst its rocky height,
Stranger to Earth, and neighbour to the Light,
Beholds its Sire the liquid desart try,
And with his broad expanse securely fly:
Wond'ring it sees; shrinks from the awful view,
And its keen eyes the hardy track pursue,
He wishes often; trembles oft'ner still,
To flutter there prepares, yet doubts his skill;
At length, 'twixt emulation and despair,
Its pinion lifts, and plunges into air.

DAY sprang I the Feigner bade her Lord adieu,
Then from a Sandal Chest, impatient drew

The boyish robe, and blossom tinctur'd Vest,
Which Osmyn's youthful Brother once had drest;
Who late on wealth, and fruitful travel bent,
Adventurous, to distant CASHMIRE went,
Where the soft Natives bid the shuttle fly,
And give to silky hair tenacious dye,
On the rich shawl contrasted colours pour,
And waft its beauties to each foreign Shore.
 Her female robes were instant thrown aside,
And as a Youth stept forth the blooming Bride;
Before the Mirror mov'd the martial Fair,
Charm'd with her figure, and her graceful air.
The manly turban next, of crimson dye,
Flash'd a new boldness o'er her radiant eye,
Fearless, she in her belt a dagger placed,
The golden haft by jewel'ry embraced;
Again, her novel form distinct to view,
From room to room, from glass to glass she flew:
 Dark crayon'd curves, then graced her rosy lip,
A spot of equal hue, her Chin's fair tip;
Self-satisfied, more gravely now she strode,
Acted a frown, assumed a stately nod.
Meantime her peering Nurse the Fair One sought,
And in the Act, the startled Ira caught;
Each to a burst of mirth awhile gave way,
And moments past in laugh, and gay delay.

SERIOUS, the beauteous Ira sudden grew,
Grander impressions o'er each feature flew;
Her waken'd Countenance with meaning glow'd,
And the Sage Matron into Wonder awed.
Think not, she cried, with dignity of port,
Thou see'st me, Abra, thus array'd in sport;
Ah, no! far other thoughts my Soul distend,
Bless Thou the measure, and the deed commend!
To share my husband's fate, whate'er betide,
Is the fix'd will of his adoring Bride.
Nay, shriek not thus, but noisy grief restrain;
Vain is thy sorrow—thy remonstrance vain;
The timid heart of Ira, DUTY steels;
Courage, and Love, sole attributes, it feels.
Duty is PASSION in a Soul like mine,
Its bounds no human language can define:
In groy'ling Minds compress'd and slow its tide,
Through Life a humble but a placid guide;
Higher its tones in minds of higher mold,
And fine the lines its energies unfold.
O! if thy heart be callous grown through Age,

Youth swells in mine, and animates to rage—
The arm which threatens Osmyn with a blow,
Shall feel what Powers from female vengeance flow
Let Men, let Heroes, for their Country fight,
Tread the proud field, and deathful fame invite;
Let Patriots rush and for their Nation fall—
For LOVE I arm, and dare the arduous Wall!
Must thy Lord bleed, and not his Ira by,
To staunch the flood, or catch his parting sigh?
Now, whilst I linger, perhaps the Sword descends,
And Osmyn sinks, abandon'd by his friends!
She spoke—a Sabre from its Scabbard drew,
And through the Streets, with wilder'd air, she flew.
The beauteous seeming Youth small notice caught,
Each bosom with its own distress was fraught;
If hopeless agony her features shew'd,
In ev'ry face the same expression flow'd—
For showers of bullets on the Rampart fall,
And wounded Townsmen stagger from the Wall.
Almost to Madness was her horror wrought,
As vainly through these Scenes she Osmyn sought,
Plainly distinguish'd, wheresoe'er his stand,
Lofty in height, amidst the tallest Band!
Yet still his lofty port ne'er met her eye—
From Post to Post they saw the Trembler fly,
Nor wonder'd that a Boy so young, so fair,
Should rush from Danger with distracted air.

AT length, amidst her hurried, frenzied flight,
One spot she mark'd where thickest seem'd the fight;
Ah, sure, she cried, if Osmyn breathes, he's there!
And onward darted the courageous Fair;
Nor vain—bus tow'ring port she raptur'd knew,
And soon his graceful visage met her view.
Now soft receding, distant stood the Maid,
To catch her tender Osmyn's glance, afraid,
Lest he should force her from the hallow'd ground
 Where himself stood, by circling dangers bound:
Where'er he moved she kept him in her view—
Now forward stept;—now gently she withdrew.
She saw him lift the Mass, she saw him throw
The pond'rous Ruin on the yelling foe,
Who, on the Plain beneath in thousands strong,
With fearless valour to the Bulwarks throng.
When the Rock fail'd, or, tired at length of these,
 The burnish'd firelock she beheld him seize,
Whate'er the weapon, still his aim was true,
Nor e'er in vain the fatal bullet flew.

At length th' Invaders, taught to be discreet,
Silenced their bombs, and sounded a retreat!
IRA beheld her OSMYN safe descend,
And to their homes th' elated Townsmen bend;
Swift, by a shorter route she flew before,
The anxious Abra clasp'd her at the door.

THE lovely Soldier to her toilette ran,
And in few minutes was no longer Man.
When her lov'd Lord appear'd, her sprightly eye,
(Which oft on Abra glanced with meaning sly)
Darted her joy that safely he return'd,
And in her welcome tend'rest accents burn'd.
A splendid feast attentive Slaves prepare,
Her Husband and her Sire, her transports share,
Whilst Music, ardent, rapid, woke the strain,
And hurled defiance o'er the hostile Plain.
Ira's soft Maids with wreathes of flow'rs advance,
And weave to sweeter notes the varied Dance,
Glide, as though Air, the element they trod,
Vanish, like forms of Air, at Ira's nod:
Again symphonious Music swells its notes,

And round the Dome sublimer cadence floats;
New nerves the Soul; calls up its fiercest tone,
And firms Man's melting heart, to throbbing stone,
Such were the notes which to his fingers clung,
When first the mighty HANDEL'S Lyre was strung;
Gigantic Harmonist! for whom each Sphere
 Its concords struck, to form his pliant Ear.
Such were the strains TIMOTHEUS taught to rise,
When youthful Ammon, touch'd by Lais' eyes,
Their fatal fire t' illustrate, and to shame,
Rush'd from his throne, and bade PERSEP'LIS flame!

CHARM'D with her Secret, the succeeding Day,
The Bride resum'd her Masculine array;
But now, the pencil'd curves had lost their grace—
Banish'd in course, from her enchanting face;
And, lest the Nurse should grave advice enforce,
Or fill with hated Prudence, vain discourse,
Successive tasks she gave the tender Eld,
Which from her rooms th' unwilling Dame withheld.
The Mirror's oft repeated duty past,
And each review found sweeter than the last;
The hardy Maid resought the Martial Towers,
And left for these, her peace devoted Bowers.
OSMYN, the Star her darting glances sought,

Soon they explored the angle where he fought,
Then as before, she gentle distance kept,
And quick as light, from side to side she swept.
Long on the Walls and Towers they kept the fight,
Thus long, her Husband safe, cheer'd Ira's sight;
Scarce conscious of the danger of the Scene,
She saw balls leap around, with air serene,
She felt no wound, she never dreamt of pain,
Her HUSBAND safe, her thoughts no fear retain!
A bold Sortie at length the Warriors crave,
On to the Gate, the spirited and brave
Rush like a mighty flood; and thence expand,
Driving th' Invaders o'er the groaning strand.
Unhappy Ira! in the rush she's borne
Her feet unwilling from the Rampart torn;
In vain her struggles—through the Gate she's prest,
In vain she speaks, her tones no Ear arrest;
All is confusion—horror—anguish—Death!
Her senses fled, she yet retains her breath.
The French now turn, and closer grew the fight,
Osmyn not once has cheer'd her far strain'd sight;
Around her sink the dying, and the Dead—
Frantic, she tears the turban from her head;
Her falling tresses caught no Warrior's eye,
They only lived to bleed, to kill, to die!
Her vaunted courage false, with Death so near,
And Ira's MAD, with soul distorting fear;
At length an opening's made—through it she darts,
Skims o'er the sanguine field, and pants, and starts,
Her shining Sabre by her right hand grasp'd,
The left, her twining curls unconscious clasp'd.
A Frenchman saw—pursued—Coward! he cried,
And lengthen'd as he spoke his dangerous stride,
Expert enough it seems thou art to fly,
T' instruct thee how to stop, my art I'll try.
Scarce had he spoke, ere the swift bullet sunk,
Pierced to her bosom, and its Life-stream drunk;
She reeling fell, then turn'd her fading head,
And fill'd her rash Destroyer's heart with dread.
He gazed, he started, at her feet he fell,
And his hot tears with gushing anguish swell,
In unknown accents curs'd his forward zeal,
And murder'd beauty made one Frenchman feel!
Osmyn!—She faintly cried; Osmyn, sole sound,
Which oft repeated, was still fainter found.
Lo! Osmyn's there. The Battle's eddying tide,
Bore the fierce combat, ere fond Ira died
Up to the spot where moaning, pale, she lay,

Unveil'd, each graceful feature to the Day!

So wan, so beauteous once Virginia seem'd,
Whilst her blood flow'd, and her last eye-beam gleam'd
Whilst roused to vengeance by expiring charms,
ROME rush'd from forth its Palaces in arms;
Her dying murmurs were A VAST DECREE—
With, her last sigh She made her Country free?

THE HAUGHTY WAR with thund'ring force came on,
And o'er the field in dreadful grandeur shone;
Osmyn, personified the aweful Power,
To his whole Band he seem'd a shelt'ring Tower;
Before his conq'ring troop INVASION fled,
And in that hour its noblest blood was shed;
But ah! the blood which thro' one Frenchman flow'd
Death, to ten thousand Frenchmen, Osmyn owed.
Triumphant, when he turn'd towards the Town,
Whose shouts, all thoughts but those of glory drown,
Of Warlike Youths he saw a distant knot,
Whose eyes seem fix'd to one concentrate spot,
"Beauty" and "Female" were the sounds which flew,
As near with rapid step the Hero drew;
The beck'ning youths still quicker speed invite,
And stronger curiosity excite;
He ran, he sprung—

No Pen bestow'd by the inspiring Power
Shall dare to paint the horrors of the hour!
IRA WAS DEAD! Thy pencil, Science! seize,
Sublim'd to madness, all thy feelings raise!
Whate'er is horrible, or deep, compel
To leave their shades and in thy fancy dwell—
Ah, throw the trifling, nerveless, pencil by,
For raging madness wears a Cherub's eye,
Compared to that which in the Bard should roll—
Or artist, who'd delineate Osmyn's Soul;
His heart would sicken as his canvas glow'd,
And agony awake as Science flow'd;
Sorrow's cold hand his powers would steal away,
His Lines imperfect rise, his Tints decay!

THE lifeless Beauty into Acre borne,
Inhum'd, and from her Osmyn ever torn;
His frantic sorrow into fury turn'd,
His bursting bosom each kind solace spurn'd;
The War—the War, his ardent thoughts embraced,
The only Scene where misery was chased,

For there once more for IRA Osmyn fought
She nerved his arm, and fill'd his ev'ry thought.
Ira!—he cried, whene'er his Sabre rose;
Battalions fell—'twas Ira gave the blows.
The Syrian Youth roused by the Warrior's ire,
Assume his feelings, emulate his fire,
Follow undaunted wheresoe'er he bounds;
One Beauty's death, gives France ten thousand wounds!
Ah, search thou RE AS ONER! when Armies bleed
Search thy vain stores to tell whence sprang the Deed!
Not always patriot fire in Heroes dwells,
Not always loyalty their courage swells,
Ambition's self not always fires their Souls,
Though their vast fame o'er Earth's circumf'rence rolls
Envy, Revenge', and Love take each their part,
Enflame the Man,—distend the Warrior's heart,
Mere private feelings public lustre steal,
And GLORY rests on Passion's giddy Wheel!

BOOK III

"What, if Ocean should bestow
"Acts heroic Deeds that glow?
"What, if ev'ry glassy wave,
"Cast on shore a Warrior brave?"

SPIRIT OF WAR! thy attributes so fell,
How, twined with gen'rous virtues, canst thou dwell,
By what strong Spell, murder to fame translate,
And make Men clasp the crime, which most they hate,
How, build thy Mansion in those tender hearts,
From which the hallow'd sigh of pity starts,
'Midst whose line nerves Affection transport gives,
And all that's gentle—all that's Godlike lives?
Ah! what a tissue is the human Mind,
The Woof so coarse; the cross-threads so refined:
Mysterious THING! who shall thy Nature paint—
Celestial Demon, and infernal Saint!

WHERE the vast Kraaken spreads his monstrous sides,
And with circumf'rence half an Ocean hides,
There wake the Mountain tempests round the coast,
Hailing the Arctic 'midst his halls of frost;
In rattling balls the atmosphere descends,
A storm of pearl each flinty wind attends.
The strong limb'd Trav'ler scorns the Tempest train,

And bends his course undaunted o'er the Plain;
Dark torrents tumble, stronger blows the blast,
From Rocks huge oaks and headlong firs are cast,
The Traveler who disdain'd now flies the storm,
And some low hovel shades his shrinking form—
Thus, bending, ACRE could no longer hope
With a vast Army's conq'ring Bands to cope,
Whose valour, diff'rent hemispheres had own'd,
Whose Arms successes had inspired, and crown'd.

EACH effort of the bold Besieged repell'd,
With triumphs satiated, with glory swelled,
The foe their strength repair'd with needful rest,
And balmy slumbers soothed each Victor breast;
No balmy sleep within the Town was found,
There Fear and Horror walk'd their nightly round.
To till the Breaches which the Day had made,
Kept all upon the Walls; the grateful shade
Which rests upon the bosom of the Night,
Here yielded to the Torches' waving light,
As harass'd Soldiers flash them to and fro,
Tending their fellows in this Work of Woe;
Flitting, their gleamy fires at distance break,
And the wide woof of midnight darkness
Streak, Red, through the black abyss of air they shine,
Taper to points, and with the wind recline.
The firm PASHAW scorning his own white age
Had dauntless dared the Siege's hottest rage;—
This is THE MAN, who, failing to be beat,
Before whose Towers brave Gallia learnt retreat,
Fill'd with immortal malice those he fought,
And rare revenge the valiant Gen'rals sought!
They seized the PEN—for useless was the sword,
And on his name their fretful hatred pour'd.
That vengeance which they could not feed with blood,
They bathed, delighted, in an inky flood:—
Charged him with sins of such atrocious dye,
As dared with those of modern Gallia vie!
Crimes which no hearts but French ones could conceive,
Which minds, less savage, learn not to believe;
From slanders framed by those who've done their Deeds,
The faith of BRITONS scornfully recedes.

THE Stars which swim above in Seas of light,
Retired amidst their Deeps and sunk from sight,
And as with these attendant night withdrew,
His wither'd Army met sad Achmet's view—
Despondence seized his soul; his head he bent,

To hide the horror which his bosom rent.
Where, were the Youths the opening Siege beheld,
Whose lofty minds with genuine valour swell'd?
For ever vanish'd—trodden in the Dust;
And England absent—Syria's mighty Trust!
OSMYN, advancing, soothed the Yet'ran's breast,
Sustain'd his sinking Mind, his fears represt;
Then through the City flew on Ardor's wing,
Where'er he moves new hopes, new Courage spring—
He spoke the Patriot, and the Hero trod,
Roused the cold spirit, and awaked the clod;
Alone the fabled Promethean ray,
Could image Osmyn's speech, its power display!
Towards the side where War its Engines placed,
Near half the City's circuit had he traced,
When, through a Postern at whose feet the Mole,
Below, at distance, bids the black Deep roll,
ELCANOR moved;—and shining in the rear,
A Troop of armed Youth, alert, appear;
On, to the Walls with bounding hearts they throng,
Not proud in numbers, yet in valour strong;
Osmyn beheld them with rejoiced surprise,
And welcome darted from his martial eyes!

BY Syria's blooming forests ever wreathed,
Not unobserving, or inactive breathed
Her CHRISTIAN Towns. Where Lebanon's high front,
Preserves amidst its Shades the HALLOW'D FONT,
Eleanor, of his pious Sect the boast,
Summon'd around him this determined Host.
Years on his faded Cheek their furrows drew,
But manly courage to his bosom grew
This Night, he cried, to Acre let us fly;
Nor here in indolence disgraceful lie.
Ah! let us emulate what reach'd my Ear!
Though England's force is now no longer near,
Its fame shall Acts approximate inspire—
We'll light our taper at immortal Are;
One deed we'll borrow from the glowing page,
Which thousands will bear down from age to age!
When REVOLUTION made its Giant stride,
And swept across the Earth on ev'ry side,
But chiefly menacing that glorious Land,
Where yet Religion makes a lofty stand;
Where her bright Code preserves its purest tone;
Adorn'd, enforced, and guarded by A Throne—
Sudden, like th' elemental bolt they sprung,
And the loud stroke throughout the Island rung:

The sacred touch each Manly bosom felt,
Each heart, where Jove of SELF, or COUNTRY dwelt;
From the soft Netts of family repose,
Instinctively, an armed force arose;
Brothers and Sons assumed the martial vest,
Husbands and Fathers wore the plumed crest,
Embodied by THEMSELVES, they proudly stood,
Guarding their Country from th' impending Rood—
Splendid effect of Patriotic zeal!
What breast too sordid its fine touch to feel!
Invasion felt it, and reverted ran;
Bearing to other Realms her dreadful Ban.

SEE! 'mongs't the Sycamores on yonder Rise,
The yellow Moon shrinks, sullen from our Eyes!
Late, when her flaming Wheel she rested there,
Safe were her haunts, and hallow'd by the Fair;
Your Mothers, Sisters, loiter'd in her shades,
And lisping Cherubs sported through the glades.
Now, struck with fear, they shun the lunar Sky—
INVASION! 'tis from Thee the tremblers fly!
Scared at thy name the timid Infant shrieks,
And its sad Mother rocky caverns seeks;
There, 'midst the gloom lulls her soft Babe to rest,
Whilst sleepless terror shakes her matron breast
Then shall not we from 'midst our Groves start forth,
And drive the Monster to its native North?
Obedient to his long respected voice,
His will became at once the gen'ral choice,
Blushing, that slumbers had approach'd their lids,
They arm, and follow, as Eleanor bids.

AT the Town's verge, ere the descent began,
Where his own Groves the passing breezes fan,
Sudden, from forth his Gates, two Maidens rush'd,
Whilst from their eyes the glitt'ring sorrow gush'd,
Deep suffocating sighs their hearts suspire,
For the soft Damsels call'd the Warrior SIRE;
They clung around him, hung upon his vest,
And pour'd their tears upon his honour'd breast;
Such precious tears rich Mandragoras shed,
On Plains where balms by tropic Suns are fed;
So wept fair Roper for her martyr'd Sire,
So shriek'd sad Hecuba at Hector's Pyre;
Chiding the wild exub'rance of their fears,
He awed their murmurs—half suppress'd their tears.
EUDOSIA like a graceful Palm appear'd,
In some young Grove by skilful culture rear'd,

Her face was Grecian, and her silky hair
Dark as a raven's, when in midway air
His plumage intercepts the radiant Day,
And throws it back a sable shining ray:
Rich strings of pearl contrasted beauty gave,
As 'midst her braided locks they loosely wave;
Her form was shaded by a thin Caftan,
Her less'ning waist to silver girdles span;
The elder this. The gay SAPHIRA'S mien,
Seem'd copied from bright youth's ideal Queen—
Though now in Sorrow sunk her lovely head,
And her slow foot forgot its lively tread.
Her limbs were rounded as by parian skill
And animation their fine' outlines fill?
Her hair appear'd like streams of yellow light
Not deep as amber, and yet more than White,
Which turn'd beneath her Turban's fleecy round,
Both, an embroider'd kerchief, glitt'ring, bound.

SUCH was the hour; such was each weeping Maid,
And thus they heard paternal lips upbraid—
If other Christians have stretch'd forth their hands,
(He cried) against those fierce invading Bands,
If other Christians on Earth's distant coasts,
Have listed to oppose their mighty hosts,
To us more sacred is the duty far;—
To Us whose Fathers saw the holy Star
Wond'rous!—Self moved!—and cumbent!—mark the Bed,
That first received MESSIAH'S hallow'd Head!
Ours is the land the blest Redeemer trod,
When in the Man, he veil'd the aweful God.
These, who his name contemn, his acts revile,
Shall these loose Infidels his steps defile?
Shall Mah'met's new disciple in his zeal,
Tear from our holy Church its modest veil,
Tread on its altars, beat its Temples down,
Which Saracens have spared in yonder Town—
Or worse! insult them with vile pagan rites?
The horror of such deeds our Swords invites!
We will oppose them whilst Life's balmy red
Is by our veins convey'd, our bosoms fed;
Go then! to prayer and holy thoughts retire,
'Tis the command of your departing Sire.
He spoke! his swift turn'd feet fly o'er the downward slope,
The youthful Band give all his feelings scope,
They Speak of glory, vengeance, triumph, fame,
Unfailing courage, and immortal name.
Heavn's azure Pole bedropt with molten gold,

In vast magnificence its orbits roll'd;
Those golden orbs saw GIDEON erst descend,
And o'er the valley with his handful bend
Tow'rds Midiarfs monstrous host "which hid the Plain
Like Grashoppers" when past a Summer rain.
Scarce higher zeal, scarce higher faith inspired
Those GIDEON led, than those ELCANOR fired;
Each Band in emulative firmness shone,
Each glorious. Chief, unfeari'ng, darted on!

To bow at length stern Acre to their yoke,
The Gallic foe in Mightiness awoke,
Sprung like the glorious War Horse on the Morn,
When on his Neck the fate of Nations borne,
Beneath some Scipio rearing his high Chest,
He paws the vale, and sweeps it with his Crest.
All bright with arms, the Vale reflects the ray,
Pour'd by the Orb who rules the hours of Day,
Whole mines of steel torn from its dark recess,
In glitt'ring horror Plains and Uplands dress,
And as the various fight the Lines impell'd,
Fresh floods of splendor ev'ry angle swell'd.
Now the big War with all its glories teem'd,
Through the thick air impatient demons scream'd;
The Bastions own'd the foe; the Turrets shake,
And the high Tow'rs to their foundations quake;
Thus Etna trembles with concussive fires,
Yet still she stands, and still to Heav'n aspires.
INVASION pour'd its Soul; yet all in vain
Throng'd they the fosse, the half-form'd breach to gain,
The Turks with jagged-rock assail each head,
And fill the Ditch with wounded, and with Dead:
Their Scymeters they use with eruel skill,
Adroit to wound; adroit in ways to kill!
Vast fiery brands whirling aloft they throw,
And scalding liquids on the Wretch below;—
A flaming shower descends—a boiling flood!
E'en these th' assailants braved, and firmly stood;
But these ELCANOR and his friends disclaim,
They distant deaths bestow, with general aim,
'Midst the firm Infantry their post they chose,
Whose double line upon the Rampart rose.

THE MORTAR'S glowing arch inflamed the Sky,
Up rose the Mischief, sparkling to the Eye:
More lofty still, the brilliant Woe had flown,
Had it, its own illustrious errand known,
Illustrious Sorrow—rustling—down it brought,

A deeper grief scarce lived in Acre's thought;
OSMYN its victim!—in one instant fled,
The Soul, which such courageous Virtues fed!
Yes, Osmyn welt'ring fell—O! Vulture Death,
Thou should'st have glutted on ignoble breath.
All felt the blow. O'er the long rampart ran,
The cry of horror for this wond'rous Man;
OSMYN is dead I in piercing accents flew—
The French received the sound, and omens drew;
Up to the Gates the sanguine Soldiers press,
Their Spirits tow'ring with assured success.
As the fell Lion on his Chasers turns,
Whilst rage awak'ning courage, fiercely burns,
So turn'd the Syrians on their foreign foe,
And springing fervors through their bosoms flow.
Osmyn's freed Soul seem'd hov'ring o'er their heads,
Still on the Walls, unseen, the Hero treads,
His zeal inspired, his vengeance liv'd in all,
Th' Invaders felt it, and their Soldiers fall.
They double their attacks, each angle try,
As often beaten, and as often fly,
Pouring in full libations to the Land,
The streaming life of ev'ry chosen Band.
The Gen'rals 'midst the carnage scour'd the field,
Undaunted moved, and round the Warriors wheel'd;
Cheering their Men they bound from rank to rank,
Rally the van, invigorate the flank;
Their ardent efforts yet they found were vain,
The bold Besieged their Fortress still maintain,
Teaching th' Invaders to respect those foes,
Whose courage, writhed with Dangers, stronger grows.

Lo! midst the toughest struggle of the fight,
Sudden, like Summer streams of midnight light,
When the blue Oceans of the Air infold
Electric flakes, and wave phosphoric gold,
The English Ships return'd towards the Mole,—
Beneath their keels the bending waters roll!
Soon as waked Zephyr had his locks unbound,
And rapid breezes fill'd the Region round,
The Britons caught them in expanded Sails,
And chain'd the vagrant Genius of the gales—
The fate of Acre ever in their view,
The gale's most rapid volumes slowly flew!
Her Spires at length come forth, her Domes arise,
Her green roof'd Palm-groves press upon their eyes;
They see th' embattled Plain, the shudd'ring Towers,
The distant space their straining glance devours.

Rough beat the Sea; no anchorage they find,
False the loose bottom, and averse the wind,
Yet still they grandly rode upon the wave,
Shouting aloud, We come! We come to save!
Th' inspiring cry was felt where LEB'NON towers.
And CARMEL heard it in her lofty Bowers,
The way of NAZARETH received the sound—
We come! We come to save! its Echoes breathed around

TH' imperious duties of the hour were clear,
And round the Headland they forbore to steer,
Shun the safe MOLE, cleave to the Western shore,
Where the War thunder'd, there the Helmsmen bore—
The crowded decks with big emotions glow,
In ev'ry voice contagious ardors flow,
From Prow to Stern the emanations dart,
Flame in the eye, and throb in ev'ry heart;
The eager Ships, as though inspir'd by Soul,
Bend their high topsails to the dangerous Goal:
Seducive Images! avoid my sight!
Nor Nymphs, nor Sea-Gods shall my pen invite
I will not shew the dazzling Naiad train
Guiding the Barks across the foamy Main;
No lab'ring Tritons with their azure hair
Nor pearly footed Deiesses were there;
THE SONS OF BRITAIN on the Surges rode,
Abash'd, from These sinks down each Wat'ry GocL
Besieging Legions, not without dismay,
Beheld their colours float upon the day;
Surprise subdued, their wonted fire return'd,
And with increasing Ire each bosom burn'd,
For now they saw the moment was at hand,
When Victory and Death would choose their Band,
Resolve which side to fasten to their Car,
And crush at once the tumults of the War.

THE English Captain, in experience wise,
Though Youth's clear beam yet. harbour'd in his Eyes,
Soon as the Ships a steady Anchor found,
'Midst the foe's hottest fire assumed the ground.
His mind capacious, forms appropriate plans,
And well th' effect of accident he scans;
His judgment fix'd, he lingers not a day,
Ardent and prompt, his acts know no delay—
Instant he bade two Ravelins advance
Their bold half Moons against opposing France,
Who saw them 'midst the sailors joyful cries
From the low Beach, by swift degrees arise.

The Boats mean while a floating batt'ry form,

Guarding the Labourers; the iron storm
Falls with incessant fury on the foe,
From ev'ry point, as variously they row;
O CHAOS! when thy burning breast was torn,
When Form awaken'd, and the Earth was born,
Why didst thou, Parent! not retain'this gift,
Why badest thou IRON its effulgence lift,
Mocking the Diamond's clear ethereal glow?
Fatal the Present, and its lustre WOE!
So opes the Basilisk its beauteous eye,
And mask'd in snowy white fell poisons, lie.

ALONG the Banks the dread Artill'ry glides,
And on the feath'ry billows buoyant rides—
Now here, now there, they point the open throat,
A deadly Mandate in each pond'rous note,
Judgment and Spirit level'd every ball,
Informed its aim, and taught it where to fall.
The joy roused Garrison fresh hopes admit,
And all with new strung nerves the Ramparts quit,
Ardors ferocious to their foes they bear,
And actions madly great their Hopes declare;
Like shrieking IROQUOIS they scour the plain,
Havock, and swift destruction in their train.
Turning from these, the still courageous foe,
Meet from the floating Forts an equal blow,
The fluid waves substantial Deaths prepare,
Fate sits triumphant, and her Throne is there!

FROM 'midst the horrors of her central Woods,
Where Night rains ceaseless down its sable floods,
Affrighted AFRIC hears the Tyger's shrieks,
When from his stretch the prey he crouch'd for, breaks.
Thus furious; his whole Form inflamed with rage;
With thirst of vengeance nothing could asswage,
The Gallic Leader, dreadful in his Might,
Rush'd, to give sinews to the falt'ring fight;
Pharsalia's Plain, or nobler Cressy's field,
Ne'er saw by Fame a truer Soldier seal'd,
The French beheld—they hail'd him as he came,
And fill'd th' Horizon with their Hero's Name,
Then check'd the battle as at once resolved
The glorious hour on HIM should be devolv'd.
The Troop he brought his confidence obtain'd
In other fields, where other Wars had reign'd;
In Italy he mark'd their vig'rous tone,

Which 'midst their brave Compeers distinguish'd shone
To drive the Islams back upon their Town,
He now inspires them—nerved by past renown.
His prompt Bucephalus, as though by Fame
He too were touched, and felt a kindred flame,
Dash'd 'midst the Syrians, flinging many a stroke,
His eye-balls rolling fire, his nostrils smoke.
High on the stirrup his bold Master rose,
His swift descending Sword incessant glows,
'Till all its brightness lost in dripping dye,
No more it. flashes terror on the Eye;
Yet still its direful labour it pursues,
DYING and DEAD the raging Warrior views,
The shrieks of Youth, the groans of Manhood tear
The shrinking organs of the distant ear,
As fall-by turns the Man, the hoary Sire,
And He, whose freezing veins own'd Life's first fire.

DARK shadows now roll'd heavy from the West,
Deep sobb'd the winds; all Nature seem'd opprest;
"Strange hollow moans swam in the troubled air;
Ah! moaning Spirits, sure, were wand'ring there.
Their still warm bodies press the cumbent Plain,
Scarce yet seems, broken, Life's imperial chain—
They hover round, but, oh! no more they tread
The field of War, or the enamel'd mead!
Still did this Earthly MARS bound o'er his Slain,
Invoke his FORTUNE and her power maintain,
Death ran before him with his iron Mace,
And mortal deeds his lightning footsteps trace.
But VICTORY which thus untir'd he sought,
Though in His arm a whole battalion fought,
Eludes his grasp, as the Mimosas sink,
And from unhallow'd touches chastely shrink.
By him unawed brave Syria kept her way,
Hers, now, the Battle! Hers the glorious day!
Mailly the ardent felt th' inflictive rod,
And on Lescalles the Sons of Acre trod;
Oft had his searching sabre found the heart
Of turban'd Warriors. When his Eye's blue dart
E'er singled from a troop an active foe,
His glance unerring scarce outshot the blow.
Both by one Sword Cardan, Lecouvre, died,
Their heart's blood spouting form'd a common tide
Boyer, D'Estroyes, sudden found their graves,
And bold Laugnier no longer danger braves.
He rose with Morn. Back from his helmet flew
The streaming hair of burnish'd raven hue;

Upon his breast the shining gorget swell'd,
Dread as the Ægis by stern Pallas held;
Helmet nor gorget could the hero save,
Three Islam swords at once, prepar'd his grave,
Half rais'd, he aim'd at One a parting thrust—
His aim fell short,—his bosom sunk in dust.

THUS toil'd the Battle 'till the Day withdrew,
And Siegers and Besieged were lost to view;
These, then return where Bulwarks lift the head,
Those, safety seek where the high Camp is spread.
Contented to have given this naval check,
The English Warrior sought his lofty Deck:
Around th' enormous Vessel's swelling sides,
The tumbling Sea in savage grandeur rides,
The head, the stern, alternate sink and bound,
As clumsy waves move heavily around;
The anchor'd Castle scorns their puny shocks,
And 'midst the crystal hillocks, careless, rocks.

DEPART! ye golden Populace of the Skies,
Who look undaunted down with myriad Eyes;
O'er other Shores your endless circles twine,
O'er peaceful Regions bid your orbits shine,
There, streams unstairid with pure reflection fire,
Peep through each chequer'd shade, and bless the Poet's Lyre!

TH' invading Powers through the wide Valley bend,
And winding, to their hov'ring home ascend;
There, 'midst the drapery of his spacious Tent,
THEIR GEN'RAL all his thoughtful mind unbent,
Whilst the mute Circle's, still, respectful air,
Willing attention to their Chief declare,—
To paint him speaking asks a nicer skill,
A bolder pencil, a more polish'd quill.
No golden torrent rushes from his tongue,
No brilliant periods on each other strung;
No lightning, rapid, in each sentence breaks,
No words that petrify, no pause that speaks,
Cool and reflective he pursues his theme,
True to the thought his words spontaneous, stream.

SOLDIERS! exalted Friends! he calm began,
Behold in me the fate of erring Man,
Of MAN!
Who less than Godhead, only, was decreed;
Creation's labour'd Work—its fav'rite Deed;
Whose line we boast descended from the skies,

As round, Philosophers and Heroes rise.
What is a Hero? What the deep read Sage,
Who pours collected wisdom o'er his page;
And to what purpose had He reason given,
From the bright Fountain of Omniscient Heaven?
The stinted draught it gave us, but deceives,
As arid Summers baulk th' expanding leaves:
The passing clouds surcharged with moisture glide,
And o'er the parch'd up Earth sublimely ride,
Some transient drops from their swoln drap'ry prest
On raptured vegetation glitt'ring rest,
But when the fields demand more copious gifts,
And the cleft soil its herbage scarcely lifts,
In vain it yawns, in vain the surface rends,
No moisture comes! no strengthening flood descends

COULD this exalted Reason trace effect,
And in its germ, a consequence detect,—
Could it beyond our sight a hair's breadth know,
Ye ne'er had blush'd beneath this Seaman's blow!
Can ye forget that lie whose haughty prow
Rides so triumphant in the Harbour now,
Is he who lately, writhing in his Chain—
Scarce can my Soul its wonted poise sustain!
Ask'd freedom? Liberty from ME he ask'd,
Bow'd to my Power, and its influence task'd;
Had I obey'd, his Honour, his Parole,
Had kept his busy Genius in controul;
These iron Bulwarks, and their rocky coast,
Had ne'er beheld this Hero, or his Host!
But, though his saliant angles press the Shore,
And the Sea-mews have heard his Cannon roar,
Is he for this a CONQUEROR to rise,
And plant his Laurels under Syrian skies?
Here, whilst your Banners from the field are hurl'd,
Here, shall his name swell forth, and fill the World?
Here, shall ye bend beneath a Seaman's power—
Shrink from the Trident at the solid Tower!
The deep disgrace should crush ye to the Earth,
For fools the scoff, and for the Vulgar, Mirth!
Behold how small his force, whilst HASS AN BEY,
Hangs with his Transports still upon the Sea,
And ere these distant succours can arrive,
ACRE itself no longer shall survive;
Her Walls be dust, her Towers shall press the Plain,
Her tumbling Turrets roll towards the Main!

THE Martial Circle or approv'd aloud,

Or, veiling discontent, assentive bow'd;
Their Leader pausing, as o'er added thought,
Again, a short attention thus besought.
To quicken Fate upon this swarthy Land,
GEN'RALS! we shall recall the hardy Band,
Who, in a hollow Square's impervious sides,
(That form which Danger spurns, and Death derides)
Ten thousand Turks compell'd aloof to stand,
Whilst rose the Sun, and set upon the Land!
Now, o'er Damascus hangs their potent fire,
But from her yielding Troops they shall retire;
There to be Conquerors, and beaten here—
Ah! brand me rather with the guilt of Fear!
Beaten by him whose fate was at my feet—
Compared to this, what Ruin were not sweet?
Nor thou CAPITULATION—hateful Word!
Shalt stain the stubborn glories of my sword;
Ne'er to capitulate, an oath I swear,
Which if pronounced would freeze the torrid air!
First will I fly—steal from th' Egyptian Shore,
Run from the Army who my name adore;
Forsake them All, embrace a Coward's fate,
But ne'er capitulate with him I HATE!

HE rose! and in his Cheek's enliven'd red,
Vengeance and Hope, Disdain and Joy were read;
The Chiefs admiring, on their Leader prest,
Who scorned repose, nor courted soothing rest,
Through the thick night they rushed, and roused the Band,
Who KLEBER should recall athwart the Land;
The neighing steeds snuff up the dewy air,
And 'midst the gloom their drowsy Riders bear,
Snorting they beat the Earth, the Night disdain—
But the still Ear their sounding hoofs retain.
On MARATHON'S dread field thus oft were heard.
When not a flow'ret by the breeze was stirr'd,
Ten thousand neighing coursers of the Plain,
Spirits of those by Persian Dates slain,
Their clatt'ring hoofs infernal speed declare,
As, urged by Phantoms, o'er the Earth they tear.
WOE to the Mortal who obtrudes his sight,
Whilst round the barrow they perform their rite!
Ne'er could he tell the deeds he dared to view,
Torments await him and to death pursue,
And whilst they punish'd his presumptuous sin,
The hoofs, the snorts, the arms, increased their din,
Till from the strong and ebon grasp of night,
Shining, burst forth the messengers of light—

Then fled the Phantoms; Horses, Warriors, fade,
And straight dissolved to air each martial shade!

BOOK IV

"Ah, no! these are not Men of Clouts—not Puppets; they have Souls and Nerves, and what THEY do is worth recording"

WIDE flew the Gates of Heaven. The Car of Morn,
On golden clouds and rosy vapours borne
Came forth; illustrious Pioneer of Day,
Who had forsaken now the bowers of MAY;
A newer Month engross'd his rosy smiles,
And newer Hours his westward path beguiles,
Weave for him Pictures in June's brightest looms,
And spread before him all their richest blooms.
Salubrious breezes press'd with odours fly,
Wafting the sweets of Earth towards the sky,
O'er the Sea's em'rald waves they dimpling stray,
And 'midst the cordage of the Tigre play.
Now from the dear enchantment of repose,
Its valiant Captain animated rose,
No waking thought shook terror on his Mind,
On HIM who spread the Sea his cares reclined,
To HIM who stored the Monster teeming Deep,
His soul bow'd down, as loosed the bands of Sleep.
The Deck received Him, where his gallant Crew,
With sturdy spirits met the Hero's view;
The duties of the hour he briefly named,
His air inspired them, and his zeal inflamed;
He knew to touch their hearts' remotest string,
And make them to his glorious purpose cling.
He spoke! the list'ning Crowds drank ev'ry sound,
And their firm bosoms with new courage bound;
The RALEIGHS, DRAKES, of cent'ries past seem'd there,
Flash'd in his Eye, and bade the Navy dare!
Seamen and Soldiers shout transported cries,
And to THE POINT He sees their Souls arise—
Caught at the instant, waved them to their Boats,
And Britain's Genius o'er the Billows floats.

THE THESEUS, prompt, obeys the signal made,
Nor shall her faithful efforts sink in shade—
No crew who ever climb'd aloft more bold,
None more deserves to have its actions told;
Not to the TIGRE shall she yield in name,

Equal her claim upon the needs of Fame!
These mighty vessels down each swelling side,
Saw their brave Men intuitively glide;
They fill the boats, eager they dart away
And flying oars dash up the frothy spray—
Upon the Shore they leap with loud huzzahs,
The rocky Shore sends answering applause.
The first great labour England's Captain gave,
By Dangers dignified, the bravest crave;
For thus has Nature blest th' intrepid Soul,
As danger thickens, awful transports roll,
A tide of glory flashes on the Eye,
They rush to wounds; they emulate to die:
The triumph of the burning Warrior's smile,
Gives to his beauty a sublimer style;—
'Tis then he treads a CONQUEROR indeed!
Soft Females flutter, and his En'mies bleed.
From such, a Corps their bold Commander chose,
'Midst whose rapt impulse self possession grows;
Whose courage, firm, assumes a placid air,
And seems most tranquil, when the most they dare.

DARK rose the Tower. Near it with latent twine,
Crept the dread horrors of a fresh formed Mine;
Crowding the avenue (a deep wrought trench)
Stood a bright panoply of guardian French;
Their pointed bayonets just peer'd above,
Thick set, and menacing! an iron Grove.
Through long tradition, long, O TOWER, endear'd,
To Time's last confines be thy Turrets rear'd!
Thy sacred, pensive, interesting gloom
Sheds tender softness! Joy's illumined room
Ne'er touch'd the Soul with pleasure so refined,
Ne'er gave so sweet a languor to the mind.
From Thence our RICHARD'S battle-axe was hurl'd,
And sent a flash around the pensile World;
Its lustre heightens in each distant age,
Spangling dull History's laborious page,
On heavy periods throws extrinsic light,
And brings dark ages forward to the sight.
EDWARD'S full glories shot amidst thy shades—
His Helmet nodded in thy martial glades;
The Saracen's moon'd banners, when he frown'd,
Own'd his vindictive Lance and swept the ground.
But ELINOR!—ah, still her sainted sigh
Breathes in thy Zephyrs; still her radiant eye
Drops purest rapture o'er her wounded Lord,
Dragg'd from the Tomb; by Love sublime restored.

When the black poison from his wound she drew,
Not tarnish'd was her Lips' carnation hue,
From their soft touch balsamic odours dart,
Glide through his veins, and animate his heart;—
Thus, when the Prophet's lip received the coal,
Strong inspiration fill'd at once his Soul;
With heavenly eloquence his speech was fired,
Not pain'd, but rapt, the holy Seer retired.

BORNE on the wings of the advancing hour.
RUIN was certain to the menaced Tower;
That Tower was FATE. Standing, it guards the Land;
If prone, Destruction scours along the Strand.
"The Mine to verify," its course to know,
Advanced the chosen Britons on the Foe;
The naval Warriors, as they move, descry
The clust'ring bayonets with dauntless Eye;
These to dislodge all Energies proved vain,
The Gauls were valiant, and their post sustain—
Down through the 'midst the English forced their way,
Nor Groves of Bayonets imposed delay!
Whilst Glory's tint upon their Cheeks is spread,
Which bloom and glow with bright diffusing red,
Their Vests with flowing, living crimson blush'd,
As to the Mine they struggling, fighting, rush'd.
The entrance gain'd, they vanish from the view,
Embrace the danger, and the work pursue;
A part the opening guard, the rest unseen,
Do Deeds deserving day, though subterreen.
Each strong support, fearless, they hew away,
And as they hew, rush back towards the Day;
The Axe resounds—the pond'rous Earth subsides,
And the proud labours of the French'derides:
The Tower FRANCE came to sap remains secure,
Its bulwarks triumph, and its Walls endure,
Still loftily o'erlook the neighb'ring deep,
And their long shadows o'er the billows sweep,
Amidst the day send forth unreal Night,
And heave their vastness on the distant sight.
Immortal BRITAIN! equal art thou found,
In the Earth's bosom, or where Ocean's bound,
Thy NAVY triumph'd in the Globe's firm heart—
Ah! what are Elements when Heroes start?

SCARCE had the pearly arm of busy Morn,
The Night's dim shadows from Earth's surface borne,
Ere from the Camp rush'd forth impatient France—
The watch-word passes, and her Sons advance.

The Siege is roused; its wildest fury falls;
Transports of valour fill the fighting Gauls,
A Band from these ROM BAUD the Gen'ral chose
To flank the Mine as the bold ENGLISH rose.
Sunk the lost prop, their dreadful duty done,
They quit the cavern and approach the Sun,
Emerging, they behold Battalions there,
To hail them, issuing upwards to the air;
Thunders salute the Warriors as they twine,
And flames announce THE VICTORS OF THE MINE!
Through showers of Ball the dauntless Heroes bound,
Whilst trem'lous Motion rocks the quiv'ring ground;
Cutting their way, each side they dart their steel,
Spring o'er the bullets, nor vibration feel!
Glorious, though flying, rush towards the Main,
Swift Death pursues, and Cannon flame in vain.
Triumphant flight! say, was it human Power,
Which foil'd the dangers of this aweful hour?
Surely some Host celestial skim'd the Walls,
The pointed Cannon turn'd, or caught the flying balls!
Thus as they sprung, the rocking crimson'd Plain,
Shew'd valiant WRIGHT, gasping, and faint from pain.
Between this World and Death—the cobweb Line
Placed as Life's barrier by the hand Divine,
His Soul had touch'd; when cordial Pity flew,
And back to Earth the flutt'ring Spirit drew;
DOUGLASS its, Minister', in whose high heart,
Softness and courage equal warmth impart,
He saw the noble, bleeding, dying Tar,
And shot towards him like a darting Star.
His wounds bound up, with caution he was row'd,
To where the Tigre's colours distant glow'd;
Soon, healing ART on Æsculapian wings,
To his enduring couch its Solace brings,
Ages' experience to his anguish bears,
In new found gasses, wrapt, and healthful airs:
Her filmy domes young Oxygena quits,
And round his aching Temples, breathing, flits,
Her novel vapours o'er his pillow shakes;—
Her rosy blooms effuse; her sparkling eye awakes!

THE British rav'lins, Gallic arms oppose,
Yet 'midst their fierce attacks the Crescents rose;
Granting their sturdy aid, advent'rous Turks,
Wrench'd the materials from th' Invaders Works;
Up to their Teeth they push, and bear away
The vain protection of the coming day;
Completed, on their horns dread Engines rest,

The Earth, "each side the Foe's approach," they prest;
Their flaming Mouths incessant vollies pour,
And their deep yellings die along the Shore.
For ever raving, and for ever fed,
With Iron bullets, or with missive lead,
Th' Invaders ranks were thinn'd each tortured hour,
As from the Moons the heavy metals shower.
That native wounds made them in Syria bleed,
That their own Arms such parricides decreed,
Encreased their fury, heavier made the blow,
With keener anguish gave their lives to flow.

BUT shall the slow, enumerating page
Trace the wild War through each destructive Stage?
Enough, each day the savage rite began,
And to the Evening's edge, remorseless ran.
WAR'S Angel trod unsated o'er the plain,
And his black wings the blood of thousands stain,
With ghastly joy his icy venom swells,
As new fall'n numbers ev'ry hour he tells!
With frozen finger OLDFIELD'S breast he touch'd,
And from his heart the ruddy life stream rush'd;
Gallant was OLDFIELD; ah! then twine his Bust,
And strew with bayes his consecrated Dust!
The Warrior fell, admired and mourn'd by foes,
His lustrous courage in their annals glows;
Those who destroy'd, yet graced him with just fame,
And wreath'd, with praise sincere, his martial Name.

THE Fleet of HASSAN, long delay'd, appear'd,
And to the MOLE his thin corvettes were steer'd;
To gain the Town before the BEY could land
His num'rous Troops, and well trained Chifflic Band
Is now the point—Point which the foe pursued,
And Heaven alone, their purpose could detrude.
Reposed Battalions issue from the Camp,
Distinguish'd glory on the hour to stamp;
Their Eyes dart hope—sure Victory declare,
As gaudy Ensigns hurry through the Air;
The troops of HASSAN are of Winds the sport,
The troops of FRANCE spring forward to the Fort!
Preying on all the tribes the flood sustains,
Rushing from distant homes, and wat'ry plains,
The tall Flamingos with, their stately crests,
Their nodding plumage, and their scarlet breasts,
Thus blaze upon the Lake's wide spreading lap,
And their red wings its whole horizon wrap:
Their splendid ranks press on the vagrant eye,

And "Lo! an Army!" the beholders cry;
Sudden they lift their wings in homeward flight,
And the air glitters with a crimson light.
"Behold an Army!" cry the Syrian youth—
An Army comes indeed, with fatal truth,
Not retrograde like red Flamingos glow,
But onward, thund'ring o'er the Plain they go.
Arrived, the work of carnage they pursue,
The War was earnest, and thick dangers grew;
The Syrians, roused, pant for th' approaching fight,
Enjoy the horror, and the Foe invite;
Swell to high deeds, smile on impending woes;
And through their ranks immortal courage grows.

BEFORE the Town, near the Foe's lofty scite,
Where their Tents glitter and the Eye invite,
A Cord of Minor Mountains bind the Plain,
Forming with blushing Vines a purple chain.
These Mountains now all animate appear,
As turban'd thousands crowd each other's rear;
Beduines, and Copts, Druzes and Arabs,stand,
To watch the desolation of the Land;
To mark which beaten foe submits to flight,
That there the fury of their arms may light,
Then sudden would their shining sabres start,
And each keen dagger meditate a heart;
Fierce on the fainting troops they'd downward fly,
To purchase credit in the Victor's eye,
Swell the proud triumph of his conq'ring name,
Divide the booty and enhance his fame.
Thus cluster on the thimey Grampian hills,
Where the bright Lochs diffuse in healthful rills
Impassive chrysolites, the golden fly
Bearing rich booty on its burden'd thigh.
Ah! shall the Muse to Lyric Scotland turn,
And breathe no grateful sigh upon the urn
Of HIM to whom was' given the lofty Lyre
By Homer struck? which own'd a Milton's fire?
OSSIAN! when hanging o'er thy grassy Vale,
Thy dark brown Mountain, and thy Moon-beam pale,
Thy broad full Sun, and ever placid Lake,
Our bosoms thrill and all our nerves awake;
With implements thus few thou'st built a Pile
August in taste, most beautiful in style!
Let no bold finger's emulative pride,
Ere hope to string the Lyre which graced thy side,
For like the bow of Ithaca's bright land,
It vibrates only to its MASTER'S hand.

WAR'S GENIUS steadily his wand employ'd,
Each side was beaten, and each side destroy'd;
If a rash I O. from the Syrians start
I O.'s as rash amidst th' Invaders dart,
Whilst subtle Vict'ry with capricious wings,
Bends now o'er Acre; now to Gallia clings.
Grave twilight's gentle mission came unblest,
No gracious slumber soothed the Soldier's breast—
Here, triumph on the Bulwarks seem'd to reign,
There, shouts of conquest deafen all the plain.
The flaming Citadel shews nought but arms,
And shifting Files as urged by new alarms.
The hail of battle rattles on the Towers,
And o'er the lofty Ramparts ceaseless pours.
The answering RAV'LINS spouted still those Orbs,
Whose mighty force each lesser fear absorbs;
The Tars support their fire with hardy skill,
The gun discharged, with motion swift they fill,
Each tube bore full upon the Gallic flank,
And ann'hilation shot along the rank.
Misguided FRANCE, Here its best Heroes bled,
And Lives profusely giv'n, profusely shed.
O mighty Empire! be content to reign
Where Sciences and Arts adorn the Plain,
Content to share in universal rule,
Nor breathe AMBITION'S ever ready tool;
Thy "Tyger heart" subdue! Spare—spare thy race,
No more be Earth's Destroyer, but its Grace!

AT length the NIGHT her thick wove drapery drew,
And wrapt Creation from the tortured view;—
More dense the sombre Power her shadows made,
Bidding each Star, and Heaven's blue desarts fade,
Yet did her gloomy fields own dreadful light,
Flashing strange Scenes of horror on the sight.
Athwart the Vast of sable æther float
The son'rous dirges of the Gannon's throat,
Usher'd in flames they keep their glowing flight,
And DEATH'S own beams adorn the solid Night:
The Sea's black surges catch his lurid ray,
And ev'ry billow foams with fiery spray,
The sinuous waves roll onward to the shore,
And as they roll along, they sparkling roar;
Mountains of aqueous flame arrest the sight,
And Ocean heaves its Heclas on the Night;
Oft on their points a hanging Vessel burns,
Sinks in the red abyss, and lifts its Sails by turns,

Unquench'd, the glowing masts again aspire,
And Men ascend on ropes of twisted fire.
Repeated on the Land fresh terrors stream—
Real are those! those no illusive gleam!
Though Palms the bright deception lift in air,
And branchy Sycamores unhurtful glare:
Quick floods of flame striking each darken'd hill,
Their rough contours with transient radiance fill,
They gush down ev'ry slope, point ev'ry line,
And each sharp ridge with pencil'd fire define,
Piercing the jetty cover of the Slain,
Revealing those who writhe 'midst grinding pain,
Here, shewing Men who heave with doubtful Life,
There, where last agonies conclude the strife.
The shriek of torture tears the ebon air,
The sighs of pain; the groans of deep despair—
INFERNAL KING! this was a Scene for Thee!
These joys not thine? what more can'st thou decree?

BOOK V

"Glitt'ring Lances are the Loom
"Where the dusky warp we strain,
"Weaving many a Soldier's doom."

'MIDST these wild horrors, ENGLAND, coolly brave,
Stood firm, betwixt the rav'lins and the wave;
In Agincourt's bold, held its Fathers shone,
At Blenheim they unfading garlands won,
Yet Agincourt's or Blenheim's mighty Bands,
Knew not the woes of ACRE'S midnight Sands.
The Sons of Albion there pursue the fight,
Seeking their shrouded FOES amidst the Night;—
Pursue as Forest Lions do, by EAR,
And Lion like, unconscious still to Fear.
Unseen, opposing Swords dread duties know,
And round, and round, their random edges flow;
Dissev'ring Night, they meet—they hit—they clash,
Stroke follows stroke, and ruddy sparkles flash,
The hollow winds roar round the troubled Mole,
And heavy hours in dark succession roll.

AT length th' attenuated darkness flies—
Lo! when the wand of day first touch'd their Eyes,
On ACRE'S late high Tower was display'd
A Flag;—in colours ominous array'd!
(Not the bold Tower, the object of the Mine,

That to subdue new effort they decline)
THE FLAG OF FRANCE wide o'er the Ramparts flew,
And stream'd its insults on the Britons' view;
Insensate Trophy! O, to place Thee there,
What gallant Spirits gush'd upon the air!
Spirits, that late flamed high with ev'ry hope,
Which moves within the youthful Warrior's scope:—
Friendship, Ambition, Love, extinguish'd all,
As from thy Staff the stricken Warriors fall!
The Tower throughout this heavy Night was storm'd,
A Breach was forced, and traverses were form'd;
Their hopes thus perfected, their labours crown'd,
With transports they embrace upon their conquer'd ground!

ROWING at distance in the shallow Bay,
The Boats of HASSAN slowly made their way
Surcharged with Troops. The hour was big with fate,
All might be lost, and he arrive too late!
The Tower half fallen, choked the subjacent trench,
And made a sloping pathway for the French—
The TIGRE'S CAPTAIN, with commanding Eye,
Sees where the danger, where the hazards lie;
Lands his brave Sailors instant at the Mole,
From either Ship;—both Crews a valiant whole!
A glorious rivalship swell'd ev'ry heart,
Almost without command away they start—
Rush'd through the open Postern, arm'd alike,
Each bearing in his hand a glitt'ring Pike;—
Shouting their thanks, the Syrians round them throng,
And hail them, SAVIOURS', as they pour along;
Prompt, to the shatter'd Tower the English fly—
Their loud huzzas transpierce the wakening Sky;
The foe beneath, aghast, astonish'd move,
As the bold Sailors waved their hats above;
Indignant! down they tear THE FLAG OF FRANCE,
And to the Earth the tatter'd rag elance!

DARING, yet awed, th' Invaders climb the Breach,
And all who come within a Sailor's reach,
Felt the strong purchase of his ready Pike,
Within the breast, or through the Helmet strike:
Nor do the Syrian weighty missiles fail,
With which each rising Hero they assail,
These, and the Pikes sustain an equal part—
That bends the Neck, this penetrates the heart;
They reel, and, tumbling down the slope, impel
The next advancing on the last who fell;
The Plain below continued fresh supplies,

And dread successions steadily arise!
So when deep Seas amidst their Caverns wake,
And boiling billows, billows overtake,
Their curling tops the frothy Monsters throw,
Against some jutting Bock's impending brow,
The Rock, disdaining the presumptuous foam,
Strikes Wave on Wave, and sinks them to their Tomb

SOFTLY majestic; full upon the sight
Of those who nourish'd on the Walls, the fight,
A mount, distinct, its native honours shew'd,
And on its Swells, carmined, the Nopal glow'd.
The name of Coeur de Lion graced the Hill,
Bestow'd in Ages past, and granted still.
Here BONAPARTE stood; and on the Breach,
Rose SIDNEY SMITH, O! for the glowing reach
Of some inspired, illuminated Pen,
To shew how stood, these two illustrious Men!
To shew what thoughts each lofty Bosom strain,
When glance met glance, athwart the martial Plain!
The Form of either prest upon the view,
And air, and action, stern attention drew.
Thus stood TWO MEN, in courage, zeal, the same,
But each ambitious of a diff'rent fame;
So the two Seraphs, heading each their Host,
Appear'd, O Milton! on the heav'nly coast,
Whilst the bright SON OF MORN with fading light,
Shrunk before ABDIEL in celestial fight,
Star treading Spirit! whose subsiding ray,
Pluck'd from immortal Courts a shade of Day
And woke in Angels the sad power to sigh,
As, hurled—He darted from the marble Sky,
Down, down, in endless depths remote to dwell
Where Seas of fire their burning surges swell'.

HIGH on the Tower, bold SIDNEY lofty stands,
Guiding th' elastic courage of his Bands;
Aloof, amidst his friends in crescent form,
Stood BONAPARTE, Regent of the storm!—
On RICHARD'S Mount, but not as Richard stood
Pouring to Heav'n his consecrated blood;
Not to protect the Faith whose glorious Sun
First rising here, o'er all the Earth hath run;
No! but to quench it in its native bed,
Where yet its rays, obtusely bright, are shed.
His actions, vehemence and wrath declare,
Your bombs, he cries, nor toil, ye Frenchmen spare
We'll force another Breach—fly to the Camp,

This day, this hour, my future fate must stamp!
See, where HE stands like some inspiring God,
Guiding a Battle by his powerful Nod;
O FORTUNE! shall no blest deputed ball,
That Ruin reach—upon that Seaman fall?
Fly to the Camp! be all its Engines roll'd
Towards the Wall; a GATE we'll there unfold,
A Gate to Acre's heart—to India's Plains,
To ev'ry Court where Eastern Britain reigns;
To ev'ry Mart her Commerce makes its own,
And her proud Traders, govern, from a Throne?
Thus pierced remotely, in a fruitful Limb,
The purple jewels of the Vine are dim,
Its clusters shrink, its ruddy drops exude,
Each branch is drain'd, and the tough TRUNK subdued.

ERE this important Day—sublime in rage,
Bad elements, and arms, and hosts engage,
Rapid, was borne across the wearied Land,
To distant KLEBER's camp the late command—
That ev'ry hope of glory he should yield,
And quit with all his bands the turgid field.
They hear; with martial promptitude obey,
Strike ev'ry Tent, and tread their trodden way.
Abana's flowery banks soon fell behind
Its noble stream by Groves of balm confin'd;
And Pharphars waves which nimbly dart along,
Whilst Art's and Nature's gifts its border throng,
Purple Cadambras, marble Cones arise,
And glimpse their features as the water flies,
O SACRED BOUNDS! where once rapt Beings trod.
Who held entranced communion with their God,
Where Prophet Poets struck the hallow'd Lyrev
And awed, and charm'd, with Heaven's immediate fire!
Lost 'midst these shades unfelt the moments flew
Whilst ungerm'd ages blossom'd to their view
Thrones, yet not raised, were ruin d in their sight
Great Empires blazed, and glimmer'd into Night!

SAD Ptolemais! no vision'd woe is thine,
No shadow'd arms around thy out-works shine,
No shadow'd enemies around thee throng,
Stout are their hearts, their nerves and hatred strong.

His daring Soul to transport almost strain'd,
Upon the dangerous Tower THE TAR remain'd,
His eye excursive all the field embraced,
His sword the Sceptre' of the bleeding waste,

Where'er it pointed there the battle burst,
Where'er it hung, an infant Fame was nurst.
Struck with chill pleasure and admiring awe,
Trembling advanced the Time-adorn'd Pashaw;
On SIDNEY'S safety Acre's life depends—
Towards the Breach he vent'rously ascends,
Seizing his robe, upon the Skirt he hung,
And round the Warrior obstinately clung. Forbear! he cried;
Oh, quit this deathful post,
Or Acre is undone, and Syria lost;
Thou art the Point at which Battalions aim,
To Achmet listen, and to Acre's claim!
The Hero turn'd, and look'd upon the Sage,
Anxious from terror—White with freezing age:
Subdued; with tardy feet he slow descends,
And o'er the valiant Elder smiling bends—
The Veteran guides him to the sparkling Bay
Where crowding Vessels tore the watery Way.
With the full tide along the curving Shore,
The boats of HASSAN flew. The eager oar
Flashes its silver to the shelving Sands,
And a fresh wind each gasping Sail expands.
SIDNEY, with feelings which gave martial grace
To all his form and lighted all his face,
Received the Soldiers as they sprang to Land,
And hail'd, and welcomed each advancing Band.
His Eye was spirit; lofty was his speech;
He strode the Guardian Genius of the Beach;
Beholding HIM the Turks caught sudden flame,
His figure new, but long revered his name:
The voice that hail'd them, animated too,
The hand that touch'd them emulation threw
From its own pulse to ev'ry torpid Soul—
They own'd th' inspiring Power, and joy'd in its control.

NEW SUCCOURS to the Foe meanwhile arrive,
And pond'rous Engines heavily they drive
The Horse, tough sinew'd, scarce support their toil,
Large drops exude and feed the gasping soil:
Slow sinking wheels the weighty Sands absorb,
And motionless remains each stubborn orb;
With iron goads, with sharply pointed reeds,
With thongs, with spears, they urge the panting steeds
Brought up at length, before the Ditch they stand,
With each dread Engine an attendant Band;
Who guide them; roll them; force them to the part,
Where weakness lingers, or where fractures start.
Those thunder at the Walls; these beat the Tower;

One flings high balls; One aims the mischief lower
This an Ellipsis makes: That, darts a line
True as the Quadrant's when with skill divine,
A Herschel measures some discovered Sun,
Or finds where Comets their aphelion run.
Ye CATAPULTS, ye BATT'RING RAMS of Rome,
Whose blows made ev'ry hostile Town a Tomb,
And carried terror to Earth's utmost bound—
What powers had ye, in modern Wars not found
And in what lustrum of your conq'ring page
Was practised force, concealed from this late age?
Names may be sunk. Great sounds how soon ye fade!
The Gun—the Mortar—Howitzer—Carronade,
Vie with strong Rams; vast Catapults surpass,
With greater swiftness greater powers amass.
Ah! could antiquity forsake its skies,
Or ev'ry Marius, Pompey, Caesar, rise,
They'd own no Engine of destruction lost,
Their sling a tube', its weights by powder tost;
Death crowns them all; sure Ruin's in their train,
At their bold voice the Turret smites the Plain.

THE modern Catapult thus Syria felt,
The ancient 'midst her earliest armies dwelt,
The Art SHE taught now shakes her proudest Towers,
And ev'ry bulwark trembles through its powers.
Ere the hot Sun with straight and downward ray,
Had marked the scorching hours of middle day,
The Wall's firm front impetuous bombs deform'd,
North of the Tower, so long, so vainly storm'd.
VAST WAS THE CHASM! rumbling and loud the fall,
The Fortress shiver'd as rush'd down the Wall;
Sudden the crash; the Bulwark topling came,
And all was dust, and smoke, and noise, and flame.
His savage waves, Potoomack raging drags,
'Midst frowning rocks, and sharp o'erhanging crags;
Above, the Oak a massy Pillar heaves,
Lifting sublime the region of its leaves.
Long it resists the Lab'rer's pond'rous axe,
By wounds at length subdued, it bends—it cracks;
The haughty Monarch of the centuried Wood,
Bows o'er the Rocks, and plunges in the flood;
The flood astonish'd to its banks recoils,
And with new murmurs through its channels boils.
Thus, the BESIEGERS scarce believed their deeds,
A pause—a graceful silent pause succeeds,
Then, lengthen'd shouts of triumph roll around,
The marble Mountains shake, and ev'ry shout rebound;

Each Victor strains his animated throat,
AN ARMY'S TRIUMPHS, in the Concave float—
Almost to other Orbs the Echoes rise,
Heaven's pavement strike, and skim along the skies!
As the thick clouds of dust their Veil withdrew,
The Town at once burst in upon the view,
The Streets, the Mosques, the Churches, all arise,
And gorge the rapt Besieger's greedy Eyes.
The BRITONS there, with Turks and Syrians stand,
Waiting th' approach of the victorious Band;
Wisely, defensive they decreed the fight,
Nor flew to charge the foe, nor shun'd his sight.
On the Pleine terre by gelid Gardens bound,
Their ranks extending guard the blooming ground;
Not all the fields by conq'ring Gallia won,
Not all the Shores where triumph round her shone,
To HER SO precious as those flow'ry shades,
Those sparkling fountains, and those narrow glades.
These should She win, England's indeed undone,
And its last thread of human greatness spun;
Faded!—extinguish'd!—all its Glory's beams,
Sure, as the current of descending streams;
The Post now guarded by its naval bands,
The tip-toe point on which that Glory stands—
Her wings outspread, half ready for the flight
Which BRITAIN plunges in enduring Night!

BUT who perceives, when the Almighty blinds?
Who free to act, when his great Fiat binds?
Perception falls before his mighty word,
Science, or knowledge, not a ray afford;—
Say then, did HEAVEN the mad'ning army blind,
And bid this glorious moment be resign'd?
The Foe resolved to rest! The breach secure,
No added labour will the troops endure!

AND now THE WAR made still and aweful pause
Such as the Wise observe in Nature's laws.
Whene'er on Indian Plains Tornadoes grand,
Prepare to pour their ruin o'er the Land;
When stubborn Trees uprooted are to ride,
In the thin element where Day beams glide;
When the brown harvest with its soil impell'd,
Is to be forced where late bright rivers swel'l'd;
When Towns are to be lost, and Man undone,
Then dreadful STILLNESS sits upon her Throne!
The Air forbears to move its liquid wings,
Hush'd ev'ry sound that 'midst Savannas springs,

The lowing Herds with prescience cling to Earth,
And in deep terror, wait the Whirlwind's birth.—
Suck was the silence which stole o'er the Plain,
Where late resounded Battle's boist'rous reign;
The Towers have ceased to echo to the foe,
Defending fires forbear at length to glow.
The air collapsing, and no longer tom
By the rude tumults of mad Legions born,
Serenely moves in undulating tides,
Loiters in spice woods, and 'midst Cedars glides
The scents of Amra-trees more fresh exhale,
And load the floods of ev'ry swelling gale,
From shades of Lotos living Music bounds',
And fragrance swims amidst the thrilling sounds
O sieze these moments, Ye who Peace adore!
Haste, haste ye Peirii from the Persian Shore,
Indigenous Angels—Dove-eyed Genii throng,
Bathe in rich streams of Odour, and of Song!

BOOK VI

*"Fate hath stretched a Net for the Day; and when Evening comes, it will be known how it hath been
filled; yes, the sober Night will bring with it the torch of Truth, and we shall see WHOSE are the
TROPHIES."*

How exquisite a task to Bards is given,
When TRUTH transports them to her chrystal Heaven!
When actions real, living Men arise,
And tangible Events arrest their Eyes;
When mighty Nations in the foreground stand,
Armies and Heroes ranged on either hand!
Illustrious Bards! when will your Lyres awake,
When shall their clust'ring strings your transports shake?
When, 'midst triumphant Chords your fingers play,
And your full Souls in Diapasons stray?
Arouse! arouse! around ye Empires burst—
Events gigantic by each hour are nurst,
O! sieze those Harps which fit Events so vast,
Let their wild grandeur o'er the Earth be cast,
Let Worlds, applauding, call your strains divine,
Angels attentive from their Spheres incline!
Then shall these humble notes no more aspire,
Nor move, discordant, through your sacred Quire;
With blushes shall be hid this trembling Lute,
By admiration awed; with sentient pleasure mute!

THE Sun's vast Caverns in the glowing West,
Rich tinted drap'ry had already drest,
Abrupt and bold, ethereal Masses rise,
And pond'rous rocks start forth from heavenly dies;
Midst these the mighty Orb pursued his way,
And MAN hung pensive on departing day.
Through a deep Defile to Acre's Gate,
A Column moved, in military state
The issuing pomp majestically rose,
And thwart the noiseless Plain its shadow throws;
The Sun behind them forced them on the gaze
Relieved, and taller, from its slanting rays;—
Dark they appear'd, and steadily they trod,
Sublime in terror, length'ning as they strode!
No brightness o'er their pendant gorgets hung,
No sheets of radiance round their armour clung,
Yet twinkling lights the turning spearheads caught.
And with short gleams the bayonets were fraught;
Their beams a thousand ways shot cross and cross,
And quivering Stars from point to point they toss.
In desarts, thus, to the sad Traveller's Eyes –
Vast sandy Pillars luminous arise;
No steady flame upon their fronts they bear,
But 'midst their gloom, quick lights capricious glare,
Wild lustres through their stalking columns rove,
Whilst on, the bright Destructions gently move;
Sure DEATH'S th' attendant of this beauteous state;
The sick'ning Caravan await their fate,
They know too well th' advancing SPLENDOR kills,
And horror unconceived, their bosoms thrills.

THE Foe proceed! Pillage and Death the word,
No hope, no quarter, mean they to afford.

Not long the charge which Bonaparte gave,
Short were the orders which his "Camarades" crave;
MARCH TO THE TOWN! Soldiers! ye need no more,
Its Walls must instant float with Syrian gore;
The Breach its generous invitation shews,
To reach it, every heart around me glows.
See, where the British Standards stain the air—
Let all the grandeur of your wrath point there!
The Roman Eagle scarce so proudly rose,
When it struck terror in barbarian foes;
These higher acts, These nobler deeds invite,
'Tis ENGLAND calls ye to the final fight;
England, which treads on lofty Gallia's neck,
Though on the Earth an isolated Speck:

Behold!—their pennon on the high wind flies,
And its bold Lions seem to mount the skies;
FRENCHMEN! where'er they move pour there your rage,
And EXTIRPATION shall its thirst assuage.
To their own Island the circumfluent Power
Which makes each angle of its shores a Tower,
Scarce so important to its wealth, its pride,
As yonder spot to FRANCE, which blossoms hide:
Obtain the Garden. CONQUERORS! obtain,
Or ne'er again behold a native Plain!
OBTAIN THE GARDEN! in that short command
Is wrapt the future Glory of your Land!
That done, remember what ye owe the Town—
Each Street in native blood, each Suburb drown.

THE precept sunk in ev'ry Frenchman's heart,
And each from habit, perfect, had his part;—
They pounce on murder with instinctive joy,
Vengeance their bliss; their rapture to destroy!
ACRE expects them with benumbing dread,
Watching their course as swifter, now, they tread;
Sees their dire March athwart the beaten plain,
Nor, as before, the Syrian bosoms strain
With bursting ardors, and with desperate hope,
FANCY no longer gives such visions scope.
They wait AN ARMY proud, revengeful, brave,
Advancing quick to make their Fort, their Grave;
Appalled they wait; they trembled at the view,
Yet still resolved what MAN could dare, to do.
Ye BRITISH TARS! 'twas ye the Mass inspired,
Its fit-fill rage with solid valour fired!
The Garden of the Fort was doom'd the Spot,
To hold in dread suspension Syria's lot;
India and Gallia penn'd within this Pale,
Hang in the balance and divide the Scale.
The troops so late debark'd, in order march'd
Through fragrant ailes which Myrtle over arch'd;
The shadow loving Sycamores invite,
Thickets of Orange shroud them from the light;
FLORA and MARS thus hasty union pledge,
And blooms adorn'd the Sabre's dreadful edge.
The Fiends, who War, and Earthly Battles love,
Joying, amidst its carnaged haunts to rove,
Rose from their Lakes of Fire and Endless Night,
Press'd by infernal instinct to the fight:
Fill'd with dread prescience, Myriads mount the air
And hovering high, 'midst Evening's glories flare,
Thence downward like a rosy vapour shot,

Or sunk unseen, upon the destined spot;
The trees invaded; on each bough they hung,
In fragrance wrapt to closing blossoms clung,
Fix'd on the Flowerets, dimm'd their brilliant hues
And glitter'd on each Shrub like blighting dews,
The scent of blood approaching, there, they quaff'd—
Hell clapp'd its dusky wings, and big with Horror laugh'd

THE Massive Column with kindling ardor strain,
Close to the Town advance the shouting Train;
There the sunk bulwarks spacious entrance shew'd—
Rushing to these Unnatural ground they trod,
O'er their late living friends they throng, they leap,
They bound from breast to breast, from heap to heap!
Ascend the Breach, upon the rampart stand,
And ACRE'S gales their glowing foreheads fann'd!
Beneath, the costly, wide spread, Garden lay,
Nor offer'd, were' their feet, a choice of way.
The winding Streets, the Domes of modest height,
Beyond the Garden's bound, unfold to Sight—
Interposition sweet! its arbors form'd,
'Twixt the throng'd Town, and Bulwarks yet unstorm'd;
Unheeded now its Founts, its. Arbors rise,
None taste its scent, its water idly flies;
Down from the Rampart look'd the eager foe,
And saw the Syrian weapons glide below;
The Mound they sprung, amidst the umbrage fly,
Ca ira their Song—Ravage, and Death, their cry!

INSTANT bursts round all that mad War can love,
When dread and carnage through its Empires rove.
Th' intrepid Foe exhausting first their ball,
With Bay'nets, quick, upon the Islams fall;
They dart upon the Turk, winde round the trees,
The shelter'd Turk his sanguine Hunter sees
And springs to meet him;—either hand is arm'd,
The WITCH of BATTLE guides him, doubly charm'd—
He who avoids the crooked Sabre's wound
Which in the Musulman's right hand is found,
Feels the prompt dagger of the practised left,
And there, unguarded, is of life bereft.
Establish'd modes of slaughter, here, are spurn'd,
Date Groves, all grace! to batteries are turn'd,
The Turks dart up, and bending from on high,
Mock Heaven's own Tempests in a verdant sky,
Forth from the clustering fruit red light'nings play
And rapid thunders scarce allow delay—
The bolts descend. Remorse! thy jagged dart

Strikes not more sure, the conscience wearied heart!
As the Shades thicken, and the Eye is bound
By shorten'd vision, Evils skim around.
The turban'd Warriors scarcely know their foes,
And aim at Those they worship, deadly blows
Unskill'd the difference of garb to trace,
That diff'rence slight, advancing glooms efface;
Where SIDNEY'S Sabre flits, they think they know,
The Gallic General's quick descending blow—
'Tis BONAPARTE! 'tis himself, they cry,
Rush through the shades, and at the BRITON fly;
No room for speech, his arm alone could force,
The mad'ning Islams to retrace their course,
He beat them off, yet gave no mortal thrust,
Firm was his courage, and his aim was just;
Then o'er the crashing Shrubs impetuous flew,
And 'midst the thickest fight his Form he threw.
Thus erst the self-devoted MANLIUS leapt
Amidst the foe, and o'er the carnage swept,
Long trains of Victims mark'd the way he chose,
And piled up Dead around the Hero rose.

DESTRUCTION, Devastation, strode around,
And rampant Ruin in each bower was found,—
Bowers where transient Quiet shed its spells,
And bless'd each Chorister that 'midst them dwells,
Now tones of anguish shake their leafy Quires,
As Man, by barb'rous Man destroy'd, expires.
Running, and stagg'ring from repeated wounds,
One, on a bed of snowy lillies swoons,
His streaming Life bestows a crimson hue,
The Lillies blush, as pale the Victim grew.
One, on a thorny rose bush falls to die,
Breathing 'midst fragrant steams his latest sigh—
The Thorns, relentless, tear each anguish'd part,
But ah! a deeper thorn had pierced his heart;
So round the Steer rich clouds of incense rise,
When on the Altar bound with flowers he lies,
The costliest perfumes mingle with his blood,
And Sweets exhale as pours his heart's last flood!
The Fountains which their rainbow jewels threw,
Lustrous, and pure, upon the Morning's view,
Resplendent jewels now bestow no more,
But dash foul streams upon their marble floor.
Defiled, the myrtle haunts! There horror roves,
Danger flits here—and Fate is in the Groves!
O, ye bold Frenchmen! where is now your hope?
How narrow'd your Ambition's haughty scope!

See ACRE'S Streets! Behold the promised Land!
But there your fetter'd feet shall never stand;
Courting your steps the Town ye fight for, twines,
And, tantalizing, spreads its varied, sweeping Lines!

PAUSING amidst the tumults of the fight,
Conviction blazed on the Besiegers sight;
Through the unpeopled paths the welt'ring Slain,
The Contest's issue fearfully explain;—
They saw that all was lost! They saw and fled,
The loaded Earth, behind, sustain'd their Dead.
Up the ascent they spring, they throng, they push,
Thence bend towards the Plain—a mighty rush!
Close on their steps they felt their noblest Foe,
And to their swiftness partial safety owe:
The ENGLISH, rapid, as o'erwhelming Waves,
Wild as the Tempest when mad Boreas raves,
Pursued their flying feet; before them dart,
Then facing turn! back the Invaders start;—
Back start in vain; Syrians and Turks advance,
Turning once more the flying Heirs of France.
Two Generals own'd the equal hand of War,
Both fighting fell; the prompt ROMBAUD'S dark Star,
Sunk him a Corse where late he towering trod,
And LASNE was borne, half living, from the sod.
Where wert thou GENIUS of DISHONOUR'D FRANCE?
What distant wrack employed thy active Lance,
That thus in Syria thy forsaken Bands,
Sink, unprotected under vulgar hands?
Behold! how fast they fly in foul disgrace!
Never this tarnish'd hour shalt thou efface;
Thy troops almost within the City s heart,
Start at the word, and vigorously depart!
Within its Walls, yet, they no footing held;
All who could run, to run for life compell'd!

THE CONQUERORS from close pursuit, return'd,
And honest joy within their high hearts burn'd.
Who can contemn, if, glowing from the fight,
Illustrious actions were discoursed through Night?
Each told the glorious story of his deeds,
Whom he withstood, and by what chance he bleeds;
Blesses his wound, the badge of future fame,
Whilst swell'd in each, the military flame.
Thus, did THE BATTLE OF THE GARDEN, close;
And Bonaparte shrunk before his foes!
The "blossom'd spot" his Army's force had foil'd,
And in swift flight his haughty Squadrons toil'd,

The troops which conquer'd Egypt beaten here,
Felt a new Power, and own'd the Demon FEAR.
With eyes that flash'd despair, and furious heart,
He saw his Legions from the Bulwarks start,
Cursed the fleet step with which their Camp they sought,
Yet joined the uproar, and their panic caught;—
Again dispatch'd the Hill devouring Horse,
Again invoked the hardy KLEBER'S force;
Whose fame had thunder'd round the hilly coast,
The dread of Acre—the Besiegers' boast!

THE SCOURGE OF ITALY resolved at length,
By art to win what paralyzed his strength;
To gain by feint, or capture by surprise,
The Town where unredeem'd, his honour lies;—
His God is Fame, beneath its crumbling Shrine
He bends a Soul:—immortal and divine!
NAME must be his, by any means attain'd,
Means graced by virtue, or by vices stain'd—
Boldly, through crooked and through strait he steers,
He grasps his Good, and treads on shadowy fears!
Without the Walls, stenching, and putrid lay
The Gallic Dead of each inglorious Day,
Squadron on Squadron still unburied there
Filled with rank pestilence the floating air;—
E'en those within the Town th' infection seized,
And Fever, raging, its wild Eye-lid raised.
To the Pashaw an Arab-Dervise, sent,
Implored, that War its labours might relent;
"Great Bonaparte woo'd the pitying Chief
"To grant for pious acts a short relief—
"T' immure their Dead, was all the Hero ask'd;"
With this a flag of truce was gravely task'd.
In full Divan the sage Pashaw reclined,
And the new exigence absorb'd his mind.
Fountains perfumed, around, th' apartment play,
And silken Net-work shuts out half the day,
The open Colonnades, wide Gardens face,
And 'twixt each interstice, each cooling space;
Tall fragrant shrubs their living scents pour out,
More rich than those the copious Fountains spout;
The Amacanlh and clust'ring Cusso twine,
Their fragrance mingle, and their hues combine.
The Doors for the Pashaw slowly unfold,
Heavy with Cedar, and intrinsic gold;
And when the sounding Valves were dragg'd apart,
On the caught glance, illustrious Vistas dart,
Strain'd through each lofty Wall came floods of light,

Pure, as the beam which takes from Heaven its flight,
Enclosed, and self-existent it appear'd,
The Walls themselves of solid SUN-BEAMS rear'd!

PHENGITES from the neighb'ring Mountains came.
Seized on the day and spread around its flame;
Disdain'd the Lettice or the Casement's aid,
No aperture its narrow streak display'd,
But countless Tubes the vaulted roof conceal,
Through which a thousand breezes constant steal.
Slender Pilasters hung with flowerets rose,
Giving the Eye both object and repose;
No tint the Flowers, the Shaft, the Base display,
All was PHENGITES; all inherent ray:
Yet Green the marble floor on which they stood,
Green, as the accacias of an Indian Wood,
Save, that a few white spots besprented dwell,
As tho' a leaf, from the hung flowerets fell;
These bright arcades diverged in diff'rent lines,
And as they turn, pellucid brightness twines.

THUS, near the VISTULA in Halls saline,
Reside the lucid Genii of the Mine;
Their Domes magnificent, their Temples vast,
O'er Plains un-sun'd, ethereal splendors cast,
Beneath the Earth another Heaven pourtray,
Which scorns the glories of the upper day.
Majestic Fanes pour down the Diamond's beam.
They blaze, and in refracted lustres stream,
The column'd Ailes to. sparkling Altars lead,
And radiant Pavement pious Vot'ries tread.
There, Seraphim in sculptured light, adore,
And Saints diaphonous, their sins deplore;—
LOT'S hapless Beauty rooted to the Plain,
Where holy wrath her turning feet restrain,
Scarce in more delicate proportion shone,
Scarce own'd her lineaments so just a tone!

BENEATH the pillar'd Dome, on ACRE'S state
Its turban'd Senate roused the loud debate;
To yield or not, to the Besieger's prayer,
Swell'd the soft eddies of intangent air;
The Yes,, the No in ev'ry light were placed,
By talents tortured, and by brilliance graced;
Enamour'd of themselves each strove to shine,
And with nice art, weak arguments they twine.
At length was summon'd to their airy Hall,
ONE whom without effect they ne'er could calf,

When deeds of mercy were to be resolved,
Or generous actions in debate revolved.
The Briton rose from 'midst his gallant friends,
And in the Sovereign's presence, soon, he bends;
Then to the seat of honour he is led,
Where the piled Sopha rich embroideries spread.

SILENCE on every Lip her finger prest',
Debate was closed and eloquence had rest.
Bold Sidney knew which course the stream had ran,
And 'midst an Islam Prince's stern Divan,
Opinions pour'd as far remote from theirs,
As England's Zephyrs from the Desart's airs.
Advised, enforced, that spacious time be given,
To acts ordain'd by Man, approved by Heaven!
Wonder'd, where duties were so strong and plain.
Debate a moment could its wiles maintain;
Urged the necessity, th' expedience shew'd,
Each sentence glitter'd, for his feelings glow'd!
The Syrians gaze whilst the bright torrent rolls,
Wakes their thick sense, and captivates their Souls;
To let the living live, they all agree,
Graves to the Dead, the turban'd Chiefs decree.
Lo! whilst the Dervise stood in the Divan,
There summon'd, to receive th' adjusted plan;
Whilst in his hand the FLAG OF TRUCE he bore,
Through the astonish'd Dome the cannons' roar
Announce the pious French before the Walls,
And each brave Townsman to his duty calls.
The treach'rous Corsican already there,
His Bombs mount upwards, spouting through the air,
Fall on the Town, the flat roof'd Houses shake,
And SYRIA'S welfare is again at stake!
Swift from Damascus, KLEBER pour'd along,
Impetuous rush'd; in force and valour strong.
Scarcely forborne his smile; when heard the tale
Of the long wonders of this marshy vale,
How oft the brave Republicans had fled,
How oft in vain their choicest heroes bled.
Resolved to shew how Heroes ought to tight,
Swift he descended from the tented height His hasty
Eye the shadowy distant Towers
And misty Wall, impatiently devours,
New aid, new fire, new hope, his Troops bestow,
And boundless spread the prospects of the Foe!

VENGEANCE and JUSTICE now, at once are roused,
And all the furies of revenge unhoused;

Whilst the PASH AW, dismay'd, made hasty way,
Through Scenes where magic Walls entrap the Day,
The fierce assembly pass through every Streets,
As wild as Tygers, and than Stags more fleet.
The Rav'lins rouse, and wake their rage once more—
The flaming Dragons of the lat'ral Shore!
Scarce had they opened ere the Gallic Bombs,
Forebore to hover o'er The City's Domes;
The Batteries of the Fort gave powerful aid,
And every where destructive Skill's display'd;
The Walls, the Gate, the Towers perform their part,
And missile deaths from every angle dart
The BRITISH CHIEF at every point is seen,
Where Order's wanted, or where Fate is keen;
He guides, he governs, he controuls the hour,
The wings of France beneath his Genius cower!
KLEBER'S astonish'd Corps, who with such haste
March'd from Damascus o'er the sultry Waste,
To crush, as with a glance, this tottering Town,
And sink its Walls through force of past renown,
Though haughty in superior tactic skill,
At ACRE found they were but Frenchmen still!
Lost in the common Mass, the common fate
Embraced, and chain'd them to an equal state;
In vain they rally, or in vain recede,
Their General's humbled, and their Comrades bleed;
Britannia's Seamen upon Syrian ground,
His MASTERS IN THE WAR he mad'ning found—
Yes! at these Walls the lofty KLEBER'S band,
Own'd the proud prowess of a Naval hand!
At length exhausted, beaten, and undone,
Once more before the Breach French armies run,
Escape in straggling parties o'er the Plain,
And safe within their Works, those who could run, remain.

SYRIA no longer now forsook her Towers,
But round her Walls assembled all her Powers;
Through Day's hot Zenith and the breezy Night,
No rest they grant, or social ease invite;
Each Eye, each Heart, each Thought are wide awake,
For deep the interest, and immense the Stake!
The Shadow which around Earth's orbit clung,
Dropt from the Mountains, and the white dawn sprung,
Stood on the lofty Rock with timid beam,
Thence pour'd more copiously the living stream,
It flow'd, it rush'd—a Universe of Light!
When transport woke, and touch'd the Syrian sight:
The touch was Heaven's! triumph each bosom swell'd,

As ACRE'S SONS th' unhoped for deed beheld—
Beheld the Foe abandoning the Plain,
Where lingering months they'd held their savage reign,
O'er which had rolled, so long, Life's rosy flood,
Whose thirsty Sands had drank whole Seas of blood.
Their Works forsaken, and encampments prone,
The next achievement is, that they are gone!
Hear it, O Asia! BONAPARTE flies,
His Tuscan Laurel at your bidding dies;
From Arms invincible the CONQUEROR fled,
And Troops abash'd the humbled Hero led!
Egypt is doom'd the future hapless Stage
For Gallic enterprize, for Gallic rage:
ILL fated Egypt! o'er thy hallow'd Land,
Why ever hangs a Tyrant's iron hand?
Primeval Source of Science and of Art,
Why must for ever riot in thy heart,
Some Ruffian's dagger, or some Conqueror's Lance,
Wild hordes from Persia, wilder hordes from France?
Doubtless, the guilt of Eden too was thine,
And KNOWLEDGE drew on each the wrath divine.
Thus through Eve's peccancy thou'rt doubly curst,
And thy last plague by Corsica was nurst;
Yes Corsica, Oasis of the Sea,
Fixes her Scorpion's tooth, devoted Land, in Thee!

THAT nothing might impede their ardent pace,
Or tempt their foe to make their flight, a chace,
Their heavy Mortars to the Sea they gave,
And plunged their Cannon in the boiling wave.
The Town beheld them winde th' incumber'd Coast,
Watch'd the last vestige of the desperate Host,
The Frenchmen march'd!—the Shore received them dead;
For British wrath pursued them as they fled.
The dreaded Rav'lins on the thund'ring Beach,
Follow'd with fire, 'till they escaped its reach;
The Guns on float kept winding with the flood,
And deluged their departing track with blood;
Round every angle flying armies turn'd,
Round every angle rapid vengeance burn'd!
The solid Globe flung 'midst th' abyss of Space,
Urged bj Attraction runs its dizzy race,
There, Rocks and Oceans light as feathers fly,
Lift their huge Forms, and bound amidst the Sky
There bright CELESTIALS oft the Ball pursue,
Gazing! as Man's wild projects catch their view,
Smile as the wisdom of the Mighty fails,
And mark grave Error as she lofty sails:

Ne'er had they seen a mightier purpose lost,
Since in th' Immense the Stranger Earth was tost,
Ne'er known a vaster fabric melt away—
Than This! the air stuff'd bubble of a Day!

THE crowded Towers of ACRE seem'd all Eye,
To trace the routed Legions as they fly.
No more their wasted Camp Day's streaks disclose,
Or on the Night the sullen watch-word flows,
No Out-post with deep tone demands qui vive?
No Pickets hid by somb'rous Shades, relieve;
The distant hum, the clang of arms, is past,
And Eve and Morn resume their rights at last.
SIDNEY! with Bonaparte's latest sigh,
On Thee He 'll bend his intellectual Eye,
Confess from THEE, deserved, his shatter'd Fame,
His flight inglorious; and his wounded Name!

DEVOUTEST gratitude the bosoms swell,
Of those who in the Groves of Acre dwell;
PEACE, lovely Empress! now again is theirs,
With all her joys, and interesting cares:
Amidst their citron Groves she sits enthron'd,
And in domestic calm her Sceptre s own'd;
They view her splendor in the Fountain's rill,
And where the Roses their soft moss-buds fill,
With purest flowers her airy form she wreathed,
Whilst all the ramparts sounds of pleasure breathed.
With Light co-nascent, and from Order sprung,
To whom celestial Harps are ever strung;
Parent of every Good which Earth can know,
From whom all Sciences and Virtues flow,
Within whose Arms RELIGION'S self is nursed,
Shut from whose smile the universe is cursed,
Daughter of Heaven—sweet PEACE! hear England's prayer,
And pour thy gifts, thy various blessings There!

He, who his Children's agonies withstood,
Eleanor valiant, pious, firm, and good;
Eleanor with one graceful Scar return'd
To those who crush'd by fear, his absence mourn'd;
EUDOSIA and her Sister wake to bliss,
Their Father meets once more, the filial kiss!
In fair SAPHIRA'S Cheek the Dimples rise
And dancing joy around her swift step flies;
She smiles, her blushing mouth such pearls disclose
As those which on her neck form lustrous rows.
Wild and unbound, her lovely sunny hair,

To catch stray hearts, to-day, a golden snare,
To-morrow, purple blossoms bind each tress,
And Fancy skims around, and forms her varying dress.
Her graver SISTER moves, a Nymph, in state,
Whilst new found pleasures, brighter blooms create;
Her dazzling glances own an aweful fire,
Though in dark circlets seeming to retire;
O magic circlets! which can transports dart,
Then strike with with'ring ray the sick'ning heart,
Speak in celestial language to the Soul,
Or all its powers with rigid beams controul!
Nature too fond bade Speech its wonders try,
When such, the powerful syntax of the EYE.

ELCANOR bends his mind to placid joy,
And tranquil graceful cares their lives employ:
DANGER apart, they rove o'er verdant Swells,
'Midst Slopes of Palm, or gently prostrate Dells,
When the broad Moon rolls high her yellow wheel;
And, as her quiet lustres gently steal,
See CHRISTIAN Towns and Monasteries abound,
Enrich the view, and consecrate the ground.
In their deep shades are heard, at Midnight hours,
Rising from forth their tall aspiring bowers,
The Hymns slow notes; majestic they ascend,
And soft enchantment to the Scenery lend;
The scoffing TURK is awed, as round he treads;
And to disturb the holy concert, dreads;
The following Night again he steals along,
Waiting, to catch the grace-inspiring song;
The wished for tones awake, sublime and clear,
He bends his head, and every sense is Ear!
At length subdued the rapturous tears effuse,
And glitter on his Cheek like Hermon's dews,
A Proselyte, half form'd, he moves away,
But oft returns, and blesses closing day
Which leads him ever, to the hallow'd bounds,
Where all his Soul is wrapped in sacred sounds!

THE BRITISH CAPTAIN now forsakes the Plain,
His stately Bark bounds o'er the distant Main;
Ten thousand blessings follow from the Shore,
And ACRE weeps when the tall Mast's no more,—
Still keep its course upon their straining Eyes,
As with applauding Shouts they fill the skies.
With fond regret his footsteps oft they tread,
Invoking joys on their DELIVERER'S head;
Point out where first he moor'd—where first he stood,

When leaping from the tumultuary flood,
Speak to their Children of his air, his voice,
And shew the Ho?ne distinguish'd by his choice!
Thus, when pale Pestilence afflicts the Earth,
And ev'ry breeze gives fresh Distemper birth,
Health's Angel, sent from Heaven, on balmy Wings,
Elastic, through the Empyrean springs,
Her rosy pinions fan the boundless Way,
Touch bordering systems, and o'ertake the day;
Earth's chrystal atmosphere her feet arrest,
Sublime she stands! by gelid airs caress'd.
Thin golden cobwebs the BRIGHT VISION fold,
And purple vapours round her form are roll'd,
Reposed on these 'midst craggy clouds she glides,
And o'er the regions of the tempest rides,
Bends to the Shores which the Destroyer wastes,
And steady through th' infected aether hastes,
On suff'ring nations her blest vial drains,
Supplies new strength, and mitigates their pains:
Her task perform'd the HEAVEN-SENT darts away,
Bearing to other Realms her healing ray,
And as she quick recedes, a shining train
Of ling'ring, precious lights, will long behind remain!

Hannah Cowley – A Short Biography

Hannah Cowley was born Hannah Parkhouse on March 14th, 1743, the daughter of Hannah (née Richards) and Philip Parkhouse, a bookseller in Tiverton, Devon.

As one might expect details of much of her life are scant and that of her early life almost non-existent.

However, we do know that she married Thomas Cowley in either 1768 or 1772 and that the marriage produced 3 or perhaps 4 children.

The couple moved to London after their marriage and Thomas worked as an official in the Stamp Office and as a part-time journalist.

Her career in the literary world seemed to happen rather late. It was whilst the couple were attending a play, thought to be sometime in late 1775, that Cowley was struck by a sudden necessity to write. "So delighted with this?" she boasted to him. "Why I could write as well myself!"

And she set to work. By the next day she showed him the first act of her comedy; The Runaway. She set about finishing the rest of the play and then sent it to the famed actor-manager, David Garrick. It was produced at his final season at the Drury Lane theatre on February 15th, 1776.

The Runaway enjoyed 17 performances in its first season at Drury Lane and was revived many times thereafter.

Its initial success, and the encouragement of the newly retired Garrick, ensured that Cowley would write more. She wrote her next two plays, the farce, Who's the Dupe? and the tragedy, Albina, before the year was out.

Who's the Dupe? and Albina encountered several difficulties getting into production. The new manager of Drury Lane, Richard Brinsley Sheridan, postponed The Runaway for most of the 1777 season. Upset, Cowley thought of an alternate means to get her play produced. She sent Albina to Drury Lane's rival theatre in London, Covent Garden. Alas it was not accepted. Albina now bounced back and forth between the two theatres for the next two years. Meanwhile, Sheridan agreed to produce Who's the Dupe? but the premiere would only take place in the spring, an unprofitable time for a new play to open.

The play brought controversy. Her rival Hannah More had written Percy and it opened in 1777. Cowley thought several parts of it were similar to her own, as yet, un-produced play. It raised her suspicions. When Hannah More next had The Fatal Falsehood open in 1779 Cowley was convinced that More had plagarised from her own Albina.

Indeed when The Fatal Falsehood opened on May 6th, 1779, it was followed by charges in the press that More stole her ideas from Cowley. On August 10th, More wrote to the St. James Chronicle to protest that she "never saw, heard, or read, a single line of Mrs. Cowley's Tragedy." Cowley herself was hurt but acted with good grace. She wrote in a later printed preface to Albina that hers and More's plays do indeed have "wonderful resemblances." And she allowed that theatre managers, who in those days also acted as script editors, may have inadvertently given More her ideas: "Amidst the crowd of Plots, and Stage Contrivances, in which a Manager is involv'd, recollection is too frequently mistaken for the suggestions of imagination"

Albina finally opened on July 31st, 1779, at the Haymarket to neither financial nor critical success.

With the Hannah More controversy behind her, Cowley wrote her most popular comedy, The Belle's Stratagem. It was staged at Covent Garden in 1780. In its first season it performed for 28 nights and was regularly revived helping to ensure a solid revenue stream for Cowley and her family.

Her next play, The World as It Goes; or, a Party at Montpelier (the title was later changed to Second Thoughts Are Best) was unsuccessful, but she continued to write and there followed another seven plays; Which is the Man?; A Bold Stroke for a Husband; More Ways Than One; A School for Greybeards, or, The Mourning Bride; The Fate of Sparta, or, The Rival Kings; A Day in Turkey, or, The Russian Slaves and The Town Before You.

Sadly, none could recreate her initial triumph.

In 1783, Thomas Cowley accepted a job with the British East India Company and left for India leaving his wife in London to continue her career and to raise their children. Thomas never returned to England and died in India in 1797.

As well as plays Cowley also wrote poetry. In 1786, she wrote "The Scottish Village, or Pitcairne Green".

In 1787, under pseudonym "Anna Matilda," she and the poet Robert Merry (under his own pseudonym of "Della Crusca") began a poetic correspondence through the pages of The World journal. The poems were sentimental and flirtatious. Initially they did not even know the others' identity; but they later met and became part the Della Cruscans poetry movement. This volume of poetry was published under her pseudonym in 1788 as The Poetry of Anna Matilda.

Cowley's last play, The Town Before You, was produced in 1795.

In 1801 Cowley published perhaps her greatest poetical work. A six-book epic "The Siege of Acre: An Epic Poem".

That same year Cowley retired to Tiverton in Devon, where she spent her remaining years out of the public spotlight whilst she quietly revised her plays.

In her day, Cowley's works were popular and thought provoking. One critic noted she was "one of the foremost playwrights of the late eighteenth century" whose "skill in writing fluid, sparkling dialogue and creating sprightly, memorable comic characters compares favourably with her better-known contemporaries, Goldsmith and Sheridan."

Hannah Cowley died of liver failure on March 11th, 1809.

Hannah Cowley – A Concise Bibliography

Plays
The Runaway (1775, Staged 1776)
Who's the Dupe? (1776, Staged 1779)
Albina (1776, Staged 1779)
The Belle's Stratagem (1780)
The World as It Goes; or, a Party at Montpelier
Which is the Man?
A Bold Stroke for a Husband (1783)
More Ways Than One
A School for Greybeards, or, The Mourning Bride
The Fate of Sparta, or, The Rival Kings
A Day in Turkey, or, The Russian Slaves
The Town Before You (1795)

Poetry
The Scottish Village, or Pitcairne Green (1786)
The Poetry of Anna Matilda (A pseudonym) includes A Tale for Jealousy and The Funeral (1788)
The Siege of Acre: an Epic Poem (1801)

The Runaway (1776)

George Hargrave, who is home from college, is overjoyed to learn that Emily, the mysterious runaway whom his godfather, Mr. Drummond, has taken in, is the same young lady he fell in love with at a recent masquerade. Meanwhile, George's spirited cousin, Bella, helps George's sister, Harriet, and George's friend Sir Charles fall in love. George's designs are threatened when he learns that his father wants George to marry Lady Dinah, a pretentious older lady who is also very rich. When Emily's father arrives to take Emily back to London, George gives chase and snatches Emily back. Mr. Drummond saves the day by offering the young lovers some of his land so that they can have a fortune of their own.

Who's the Dupe? (1779)

Granger, a captain, arrives in town to see his lover, Elizabeth. Her uneducated father, Abraham Doiley, has promised her hand to the most educated man he can find, an unappealing but intelligent scholar named Gradus. Elizabeth's friend Charlotte, who fancies Gradus for herself, persuades Gradus to act more fashionable and less bookish so that he can win Elizabeth's heart. Doiley is not impressed by the new Gradus; meanwhile, Granger presents himself to Doiley as a scholar so that he can win Elizabeth's hand. Granger and Gradus square off against each other to see who is the more educated, and Granger wins by using phony Greek that nonetheless impresses Doiley. Gradus is consoled by winning Charlotte.

Albina (1779)

The powerful Duke of Westmorland learns that the gallant young soldier Edward is in love with his daughter, Albina, who is a young widow to Count Raimond. Despite her love for Edward, Albina's virtue impedes her from agreeing to marry him. Westmorland and Edward persuade her to remarry because Edward is soon destined to go off to war; she agrees. Editha, who is jealous of Albina, seeks help from Lord Gondibert, Raimond's brother, who secretly loves Albina. On the eve of the wedding, Gondibert tells Edward that Albina has been unfaithful, and to prove it he disguises himself and allows Edward to spy on him sneaking into Albina's chamber at night. Edward then calls off the wedding, and the furious Westmorland challenges him to a duel to protect Albina's honour. Before the duel begins, Gondibert's elderly servant, Egbert, exposes his master's lie, and the king banishes Gondibert. Before he leaves, Gondibert vows to kill Albina and then commit suicide. He sneaks into Albina's chamber and stabs a woman he thinks is Albina, and then he stabs himself. But the woman turns out to be a disguised Editha, who had also stolen into the room. Edward is relieved when the real Albina rushes into the room, and the dying Gondibert asks for and receives her pardon.

The Belle's Stratagem (1780)

Having returned from his trip to Europe, the handsome Doricourt meets his betrothed, Letitia. He finds her acceptable but by no means as elegant as European women. Determined that she will not marry without love, Letitia enlists the help of her father, Mr. Hardy, and Mrs. Racket, a widow, to turn Doricourt off the wedding by pretending that she, Letitia, is an unmannerly hoyden. Meanwhile, Doricourt's friend Sir George is being overprotective of his new wife, Lady Frances, who rebels and agrees to accompany Mrs. Racket for a day in the town and a masquerade ball that night. While out at an auction, Lady Frances meets the rake, Courtall, who brags to his friend Saville that he will seduce her. Meanwhile, Letitia's brazen acting succeeds in dissuading Doricourt from wanting to marry her. All characters converge at that night's masquerade. The disguised Letitia shows off her charms, bewitches Doricourt and then leaves before he can find out who she is. Courtall, disguised the same way as Sir George, lures the lady he thinks is Lady Frances back to his house. However, Saville has replaced the real Lady Frances with a prostitute who is disguised as Lady Frances is. Shamed, Courtall leaves town. The next day, Doricourt, who has been told that Mr. Hardy is on his deathbed, visits him and reluctantly agrees to marry Letitia after all. Then the disguised Letitia enters and reveals her true identity to the overjoyed Doricourt, who also learns that Hardy was not ill after all.

A Bold Stroke for a Husband (1783)

Set in Madrid, the play tells of Don Carlo, who has fled his wife, Victoria, for the courtesan Laura. Laura breaks off with Don Carlo, but she holds on to the documents that entitle her to his land, a gift he foolishly gave her. We learn that Laura is in love with Florio, who is really Victoria disguised as a young man. Meanwhile, Victoria's friend Olivia is resisting efforts by her father, Don Caesar, to marry her off to a series of suitors. In desperation, Don Caesar pretends that he will marry and young girl and then send Olivia off to a convent unless she marries right away. Victoria persuades Olivia's servant to disguise himself as her rich uncle, the original owner of the land that Laura now holds. He convinces Laura that the titles are worthless, so in a rage she rips them up. Victoria reveals herself to Don Carlos, who repents and pledges himself to her again. Meanwhile, Olivia gets married to Julio, the man she wanted all along.